Yesterd

An Anthology of
COVENTRY IN LOCKDOWN

Chosen by Cathy Cassidy

Fair Acre Press

Published by Fair Acre Press in 2020

www.fairacrepress.co.uk

A CIP catalogue record for this title is available from the British Library.

ISBN 978-1-911048-48-0

Front Cover image © Tara Louise Malocco 2020
Cover design and Typesetting by Nadia Kingsley

Sitting Rooms of Culture

Sitting Rooms of Culture was set up by four Coventry artists as a grassroots response to the Covid crisis, using creativity to support local artists and the wider community, during lockdown – and beyond. The Group showcases the abundance and diversity of creativity in Coventry and Warwickshire – revealing many talents that have been hidden under the carpet until now. You can find the group on Facebook and are very welcome to share your creations there.

Sitting Rooms of Culture Founders:
Mary Courtney, Kirsty Brewerton, Paul Curtis, Heather Davison

Thanks to all who submitted work for the
Coventry Couch Potato Challenge 2020,
published or not... your work came from the heart
and every word was appreciated.

Apologies to those we have been unable to contact – we did try.

Acknowledgements

Many thanks to each and everyone who made this book come to life:

All the contributors who joined in the Couch Potato Writing Challenge, all the volunteers who gave so generously of their time. Huge thanks to Cathy Cassidy for her care and commitment in selecting and putting the biographies and compilation together. Sitting Rooms of Culture for daring to want this book to happen. Mel Beech, Walter W Milner, Phil Tutchings, Jeanette Tilley, Clare Allington-Dixon, Andrea J Cox and Charlotte Lewis, for preparing the manuscript. Aimie Brewerton, Filippo Cuttica and Ben Mellor for Couch Potato design work. Paul Curtis, for promoting the writing challenge, and to all those who supported getting the word out: Mandy Crilly from Coventry Libraries, Dave Copson, Martyn Yeo, Amy Cobbett, Chris Courtney, and many other teachers and friends, along with Daksha Priparia from Foleshill Creates, Echo community newspaper, Coventry Telegraph, Coventry Observer, Raef Boylan, Andrea Mbarushimana and many of the Coventry poets, Chloe Deakin, Coventry and Warwickshire Chamber of Commerce, and the Students' Unions. For the radio coverage thanks go to Paul Sanders from Hillz FM, Siobhán Harrison, Rachel New and Lorna Bailey from BBC CWR and Neil and Gaylita Bradley, Coventry Arts Collective Ltd., for the Abbey Radio air time. Kirsty Brewerton for launching the Crowdfunder and Kath Lole for the admin. Thanks to our anonymous benefactor and everyone who made a donation to help make this book happen. Tara Malocco for the wonderful drawing. Nadia Kingsley of Fair Acre Press for her attention with the publishing and all the pre-publication support. Mary Courtney for instigating and organising.

Cathy Cassidy

Tile Hill born and bred, educated by Coventry libraries and one-time art teacher at her old secondary, Bishop Ullathorne, Cathy is now a bestselling children's author. She likes to encourage people of all ages to follow their creative dreams, and although now based in North Wales she has huge affection and respect for her old home city.

Cover image by Tara Louise Malocco

'Hi. I'm Tara Malocco. I'm a mum of two lovely girls. I've been associated with Coventry for over 10 years. I trained as a nurse at Coventry University and now work at the Coventry Health Centre. I took up drawing as therapy for my mental health during lockdown - and now have got a massive love for art.'

Thanks to Michael Mogan MBE for sponsoring this book

'As a Coventry resident who has worked as a fundraiser for scores of good causes, including the city's cathedral and the City of Culture campaign, I'm pleased to support this book as it seeks to celebrate the skills of our city's fine writers.'

Contents

Foreword

Hello,

Way back at the start of lockdown, I was asked to head up a writing challenge that would encourage would-be writers and poets in the CV postcode area to share their feelings about the Covid-19 crisis in a creative way. The idea was that a selection of the resulting pieces could be collected in book form, a record of Coventry's experience of the lockdown.

Sitting Rooms of Culture, a Facebook group and initiative to get Coventry folk in quarantine to dig deep, find their hidden talents and explore their imaginations, were the instigators. *'Can we get a sofa into it?'* they asked. 'We're all stuck at home now, in our sitting rooms, right?' I didn't want to ask people to shoehorn a sofa into their pieces, so came up with the idea of calling the project the "Coventry Couch Potato Challenge". Lockdown had turned us all into couch potatoes, after all, and the challenge was to get off that couch, spread our wings and fly.

Together we launched the challenge, and in came the stories and poems – just a few at first, and then more and more as the news spread. Hundreds. Gulp. The closing date passed and I began sifting, choosing, editing, collating. It took six or seven weeks longer than the fortnight I had optimistically planned for, but I was blown away by the diversity, the quality, the wit, humour, honesty and emotional impact of what I was reading.

There were entries from accomplished, published poets, from children and teens and mums, dads, grandparents. There were pieces from frontline NHS workers, from key workers of all kinds, from the furloughed, the quarantined, the shielding, the angry, the frightened, the bored, the lonely. Some pieces made me laugh, some made me cry, many made me think and some offered blissful escapism or searing realism. All human life was here, and it was awesome.

Thank you, people of the CV postcode, for baring your souls in this way, and for allowing me to work with you to create this book. I've tried hard to do my best for each piece of work, but these days I'm no longer a fiction editor or proofreader and my work on this project was done on a voluntary basis, fitted in between my regular work and family commitments. If there are mistakes, they're likely to be mine.

I hope it's not too much of an imposition to include my own short story, because although I no longer live in my old home town, I have thought of it often throughout the lockdown.

Yesterday's Diary – the title comes from a lovely prose piece by contributor Gill Yardley – reflects the range of feelings, experiences and emotions of Coventry under lockdown.

Pieces are scattered throughout the book, deliberately not themed or segregated by age, occupation or status. This is a book to dip into over and over, with something for everyone. Take a look through, read a story, a poem, and allow yourself to remember the difficult lockdown days of 2020.

Cathy Cassidy

Coventry-born children's author

Ghost Town

Someone wrote a song about it once, and everyone was divided on whether it was about Coventry or not. Maybe it was every town, back then... lost, forgotten, shops closed up. We never imagined it could ever happen for real, but hey, that was just one of the tricks that 2020 had up its sleeve.

It's a long time now since I've lived in Coventry, but lately when the lockdown boredom bites I am back there again, the place that made me, the place where I began.

I'm three years old and dangling a toy fishing net into the Swanswell, out with my best friend Keith-From-Next-Door and his lovely mum. An older boy catches a stickleback in a jam-jar and pokes it with a stick, and outraged I grab the jam-jar from him and throw the fish back into the water.

I'm five years old and in town with my mum, riding on the roundabout by the birdcage, peering at the cake display in Elizabeth the Chef, watching the lady lift a cream horn and place it in a box to take home for Dad. Mum and I have a pineapple tart to share. The box is tied up with ribbon and Mum puts it in her shopping basket, and we go to British Home Stores to buy cheese before catching the bus home. I think I'd like to be a cheese lady when I grow up, slicing things with that shiny wire and wrapping them in paper.

I'm nine years old and racing across the playground at Our Lady's, chanting skipping rhymes, spinning in and out of the elastic when we play French skipping, doing handstands up against the wall behind the bins. Once we sit all lunchtime in the church, watching the statue of Our Lady because Deborah says she's seen it cry. We watch until our eyes go blurry and start to ache, and then someone says the statue smiled instead and we go back to our games, satisfied.

I'm eleven years old and off to town on the bus by myself for the first time ever. I meet Siobhan at Broadgate and we go to Boots and buy identical purple eyeshadows that come in a push-up tube, like lipstick. We go to the ladies toilets and paint stripes of purple across our eyelids and dream about being grown up, sad because we'll be going to different secondary schools.

I'm thirteen years old, painfully shy in my smiley t-shirt and flares, collecting this week's Jackie magazine from the paper shop. I call into the corner shop to get potatoes for Mum, blushing scarlet because the flirty boy with wavy blond hair is serving.

I'm fifteen years old, drifting along the bookshelves in Tile Hill Library, the old breeze-block one that doesn't exist anymore but is forever windswept and grey, immortalised in a painting by George Shaw who went to school with my little brother. I'm in Earlsdon Library too, and up in the galleries of the old Central Library with armfuls of art books and a head full of dreams.

I'm at dozens of sixth form parties at the St Brendan's Club and the upstairs rooms of pubs long since demolished, winning a goldfish at the fair on the common, shivering in a swimsuit outside the swimming pool that time they had a bomb scare, standing outside the fur coat shop with my mum to smell the coffee roasting in the shop tucked away behind it, because we loved the smell even though we didn't like fur coats, or coffee.

I am everywhere in this city, and nowhere. I mooch through the precinct in my brown flared dungarees and I can almost see the tumbleweed rolling past the Rotunda, because right now it's only us ghosts who haunt the streets of Coventry.

I'm not alone, of course. I see the ghost of my mum, a kid walking home from the big air raid shelter on Broad Lane the morning after the Blitz, trying not to cry. It was her birthday and she knew there'd be no cards because there was no anything, not any more. I see the ghost of my dad, roaring as he rode a home-made go-kart down the steep hill of Devil's Dungeon. My grand-mother, queuing for rations, my grandad watching for fire on the rooftops of the Massey Ferguson factory even as my other grandad sits in their office designing fighter plane engines. My nanna's ghost bakes jam tarts and gets lost on city buses for all eternity, and that's just my family, of course.

There are so many of us... Coventry kids from across the years, the centuries, our lives woven in and out of this place like spiders' webs. When the city is silent and empty, our wraiths shimmer bright in the hot May sunshine.

You're not alone, I promise. We're all here, together, still.

Cathy Cassidy
I'm a children's author, born and raised in Coventry and privileged to have been asked to lead this lockdown writing challenge. I now live in N Wales with my husband and I have two grown-up children. This story is my lockdown love letter to Coventry.

Yesterday's Diary

March 29th

All appointments – some exciting ones – in my day-to-day diary have been cancelled till further notice. This distresses me. Getting bored now. I washed a lot of things that were hanging round. Now they are hanging around on the line. Found a Christmas pudding in the cupboard… it will be great for Easter. Made almond biscuits. Instructions said 'First crush your almonds,' but they ricocheted all over the kitchen floor that had just been swept. They didn't crush up much and are hard and bitty. Worried I might break a tooth (are dentists open?) Biscotti is too posh a description, but you get my gist.

Allowed out for shopping – first time in three weeks for us. Stood behind black and white tape in a queue till our turn came. Watched The Nest on playback. Sinister teenager fleeces desperate couple. It promises to get even more sinister. Followed this with Dad's Army for some light relief.

In the absence of garlic for my mince, found wild garlic in the garden. Reminisced about buying the plant last summer on a day out. A day out – there's a thing. Roll on next summer. Avoiding watching the news, so does anyone know how Boris is?

Went for a walk and waved to people. I am in a completely slowed down world. Had shower and cocoa, then a nice read of my second library book. Only got four more. What then? I want the new Anne Tyler and Lady Glenconner's book, and there's an Anne Enright I haven't read. Guess I have to dream on. Feeling well and rested though.

April 2nd

Had a pleasant shop at Asda yesterday. Staff have always been friendly in there, but yesterday they excelled themselves. Both of us hate the self-service machines if we have more than two items, which we did. 'Unexpected item in baggage area' sends a chill through me as we often do it wrong. Lovely lady did it all for us, and all with a smile. Well done and thank you, Asda Jubilee Crescent.

Next, a little bit of gardening to remove the uninvited Spanish bluebells and ground elder. Thought of Lady Macbeth and the hand washing, 'out, out damned spot.' Saw Julie Walters play this part at the Leicester Haymarket in the 1980s. She was wonderful at washing her hands in a very anguished way. Always had a soft spot for Julie. Didn't you just love her singing 'Take a Chance on Me' in her wobbly, gentle way in Mamma Mia? Nice telephone call with Carol, and a lovely photo of Marta's new baby nephew, one day old. Had a curry and watched some telly.

April 4th

Another sunny day, a day to spread out in and potter about a bit. Our house and garden are benefitting.

'Home Thoughts from Home.'

Oh to be in England, now that April's here,
and whoever wakes in England sees some morning, well aware,
the world has changed beyond belief, there are no people on the heath,
and to the frontline workers we must bow, in England, now.

Apologies to Robert Browning.

We will be out there at 8pm banging the gong and clapping for front line workers. Will you?

April 10th

Beginning to see some plusses in this isolation lark. So many body swerves whilst out walking – it must be doing my spare tyre some good. People being cheery and smiling a lot now they have time to take time. Let's hope that lingers when we are at last allowed out.

There are more rainbows in windows, wonderful. Continued sprucing up the bedroom skirting boards but it may become a thing of the past as white paint flakes are coming off here and there. Redecorating is not on our list of things to do soon.

Moving Gran's mahogany chest of drawers I found a Turkish five Lira note. Remembering that it was 30,000 lira for a Cornetto in 2006, I'm not about to transfer into an ISA before it's too late as they keep telling me to.

Fishy day too. It was sardines on toast for lunch and plump cod from Morrisons for dinner. Managed to watch a superb Art Nouveau programme on playback. Pity Montalbano was a repeat.

Poured a glass of Muscadet then played the Belgrade Shakespeare quiz pointed out for me by Mike Howard, which I'd recommend, thanks to them for doing this. Who knew Falstaff was in three plays? Not me. Pleased to get Coriolanus and the

Timon one. Failed with Mark Anthony. I am in awe of other people's knowledge of The Bard. Watched Celebrity Bake Off – very funny. Alex broke a bowl, and there were two cut fingers.

Tomorrow is another day in captivity.

April 23rd

Today is Shakespeare's 456th birthday and also St George's Day, that is the order I think of them – apologies to the patriotic from an avid theatregoer. Shakespeare has given me a lot of pleasure in my life, not to mention so many apt quotes for every occasion. In Macbeth, Ross says: 'Things at the worst will cease, or climb upwards, to what they were before.'

I really do hope so. Let's pray by April 2021, his 457th birthday, we are lining the streets of Stratford with our posies of rosemary, actor and dignitary spotting, as we have done before so many times, and that life has somehow recovered from this current plague.

I'm finding there can be isolation irritations. Like Himself exercising in the kitchen in front of my cooker when a cake is ready, or having to share the trowel at the same time, whilst gardening. A dismal lack of flour, eggs, and dried fruit in the shops. People checking who is slipping out when they shouldn't be. For goodness sake!

For us there is quite a big upside though. Meals are more leisurely, planned and seemingly tastier, too. Despite trowel envy when the other is using it, our garden looks a treat. Every hour spent tending is rewarded with treasures.

Oh – and sleep. Getting the full eight hours most nights. Waking up free of previous worries is priceless. Phone calls are lovely now, not in the least intrusive, as they could sometimes seem before. Apologies for being Pollyanna again.

April 28th

So, Boris is back, bringing with him a sort of John Bunyan Pilgrim's Progress message. There's certainly no discouragement that will make him relent on lockdown. I applaud that and admire his strength of resolve. We are making progress. Armed with the shield of lockdown and the sword of face masks, we are on our way to mugging this virus back.

I'd be pleased at the progress of the blond pilgrim and his cohorts as a whole, if only it wasn't overshadowed by the over-70s yardstick. This is personal. Common sense must prevail, and the date on my passport shouldn't condemn me to a restricted life in future. So much to do, life to live, people to meet, places to go! End of rant!

The garden is looking great apart from the thugs. Spanish bluebells with their luxuriant foliage have been removed. There's a sort of yellow poppy, though, which is sweet... but it lays roots under everything and bobs up in the middle of things like Moses in the Basket and Alchemilla Mollis, which I feel will be lost to this interloper. It's the cuckoo of the garden world. So, fork and trowel at the ready, I'm coming to get you – cute or not.

May 29th

It seems that we are moving on. From next week we can barbecue a six not a deux! And it was the last clap for carers, too, last night. Half of our close joined in enthusiastically, which is better than none! This re-entering the world's stage is an odd one. Still restrictions in place but no map on how to deal with some situations.

One of the things I miss is my days out with my oldest son. We would have lunch, his treat, and then go to the cinema to see a good film. Or we'd get on a train to Birmingham and then the tram, and explore the Black Country. Bilston was always a good bet. We'd begin at St Leonard's church cafe for coffee and crumpets, then hit the town – market first, then on to the Henry Newboult for a gin (me) and a beer (him.) That has finished now – we are unimpressed by how staff at Wetherspoons were treated at the start of this crisis, so now it would be the Trumpet by Lidl, then Majors for fish and chips. They do the chips with blobs of golden batter on – wonderful.

What a trying and scary time it has been. I can't imagine how lonely and frightened people must have been, and my heart goes out to the carers for whom there was no respite. This virus is vulgar, with no morals. That's all.

Gill Yardley

I am retired, happily married, and life is full and interesting – I am part of the Belgrade Theatre Elders company, bringing opportunities I never dreamed I'd have. I've been writing seriously since my twenties – I'm 75 now, and it still gives me pleasure.

Lady Godiva in Lockdown

'Stay at home,' she told them,
'Do as you've been told.
Stay inside behind closed doors.
Don't peep, don't be so bold.

For I've heard of your plight,
your shortages of food,
and my husband says he'll make it right
if I ride round Coventry nude!

I've pled your cause so many times
so now I'll have to go.
I just can't stay home making bread
when you're sour about the dough.

Fear not, the salons are all shut
so now my hair is grown.
It's long enough to clothe me and
I'm bored of baking scones.

In fact, I would quite welcome
the chance to exercise,
so will ride out upon my horse
to keep you in supplies.

I will leave Leofric behind
to homeschool for the day;
he can deal with our nine kids
while I ride on my way.

So please do stay at home for now,
distant, out of harm's way,
obscure the view with rainbow signs
and soon we'll be ok.'

Alison Manning

I've lived or worked in Coventry most of the time since coming here to study English at the University of Warwick last century. My spare time is spent on church and community activities, reading, going for walks with my family, thinking about writing, but not often getting round to it, and trying to grow lemons.

1977

This is all my fault. I asked for it. Well, I asked for something to happen. It was February of 1977, I was just waking up to the sound of punk rock and that my life was dismal. Really dismal. The results from my mock O levels were tragic; I was the only one in the year who was not going to take English Literature.

I'd had a brain freeze in the exam and spent the whole time answering questions and writing lengthily and floridly on Wilfred Owen and the War Poets and as it neared the end of time, I smugly put down my pen and looked round smiling at all the hapless wits who were still working away. Just to be on the safe side, I read the question paper back again and on the front it clearly said in capital letters: YOU MUST ANSWER ONLY ONE QUESTION FROM EACH SECTION. It hit me like a hammer and as I grabbed my pen to furiously scribble how much I loved Billy Casper in A Kestrel for a Knave and how the only thing that dragged him from the sadness and despair around him was Kes and that was how I felt about music and I know I was living in suburbia and not the Barnsley mines but the struggle was real and I was oppressed and 'PENS AND PENCILS DOWN!' bellowed forth and I was undone.

Later, I sat on the bus reading a Pan Book of Horror Stories; my hair was greasy, I was excruciatingly shy, Sharon Timmins had suddenly stopped talking to me after I unexpectedly and dramatically broke wind in games, I would not get into college so had to get a job in July and on the end of my nose, the very end, was an inflamed red spot ready to blow like Krakatoa at any minute.

In the short story I was reading, a monkey's paw was gripped tightly and wishes were asked only for grimness and death to follow. What could possibly go wrong? I closed my eyes while tightly gripping the book. 'Monkey's paw, allow me this wish. Stop school, stop everything, stop the world... make us stay at home, just leave me alone in my bedroom to learn to play guitar like Mick Jones. Give me time for this bloody zit to explode and go away, cancel the exams, and somehow get me into college so I don't have to work. Oh, and if you could stop me from blushing all the time and get Sharon Timmins to talk to me again, that would be great.'

Of course, nothing happened. There was no clap of thunder, no fireworks and the 182 bus trundled on home. I did disastrously in my exam, my hair continued to be greasy, Sharon never spoke to me again, I had to find a job and the zit on my nose exploded over Penny Saunders in the middle of Knowle Village Hall disco as I was pogoing to Pretty Vacant.

And now, fast forward to today. The schools are closed, exams are cancelled, I can stay in as much as I like, my hair is pretty amazing for a bloke touching 60, I can get a few tunes out of a guitar and I haven't had a zit on my face since Sid Vicious died.

Do wishes have a time limit?

Oh God, what have I done?

Nick Knibb

hope

there is always hope.
who'd have thought that the thing that would bring us together
would be the same thing that was keeping us apart?
we stood that evening and watched the sky as the space station went by
and wondered what on earth do they think of this mess?
hermetically sealed and out of reach
drifting up there in their own world of peace.
during the day the sound of the A45 is muted
and as the sun comes up flymos and strimmers are brought out of sheds
to puncture the birdsong
and as this new normality carries on

I sit back and remember the strangest of times...
here on this table I wrote a shopping list
and then crossed out all the things they didn't have in the Co-op
and started to look quizzically at unnamed tupperware in the back of
the freezer
at something that could be peaches or butternut squash
and wondering if Jamie Oliver ever had this conundrum.

out there in the garden is where I planted the seeds
'well at least we'll have lettuce and potatoes to eat
in the summer,' I said
in this shadow I sat under the big tree
and thought about all the things I was going to do
all the things I was gonna be
and on this bench six weeks later I sat in the sun
and remembered all the things I still hadn't done.

we let the earth breathe again for a fraction of time
and cleared the skies
and found that sometimes it was nice just to sit and listen.

we learned how to be human and speak to our neighbours
we opened gates and nodded and thanked and waved
as the bashful bin men were greeted like heroes
and carried on as before.

there is always hope
and those who've dragged us through it
holding together as we fell apart
deserve the dawn of a new age when importance of their position
is recognised with distinction
and to not be ignored at the ballot paper
and rewarded with something more substantial than a round of applause.

there is always hope

Nick Knibb

here

this place is built of stronger stuff than bricks and mortar iron and mud
and like a hand fits into glove we know that we are here
and when we look on halcyon days now that life has slipped out of phase
and something new is in its place we know that we are here
parallels drawn of darker nights and flattened houses and firelit skies
always in our hearts and minds we know that we are here
from black and white and sky-blue blood this is our neighbourhood
and with a grace from up above we know that we are here

and now we think it an oddity
when wealth not health is considered a commodity
and frozen like never before we sit and watch TV
and the news from day to day blurs into one facts and figures run and run
and the skies grow quieter and the birds get louder
as their glorious domain
grows prouder and prouder
and a silent menace one we can't see as the nurses are searching for PPE
and the news on the radio gets worse and worse so they try to persuade
you to commit it to verse
and we spend all day in pyjamas and tees and scream at the sound of
microsoft teams
so I'll close my eyes and drift back to a time when the most important
thing on my mind
was packed into crates at record shops
and I dreamt of being on Top of the Pops
and the news commentary comes from room to room in pixelated skype
or fuzzy zoom
and you hope that it'll be over soon before it reaches your door

this place is built of stronger stuff than bricks and mortar iron and mud
and like a hand fits into glove we know that we are here
and when we look on halcyon days now that life has slipped out of phase
and something new is in its place we know that we are here
parallels drawn of darker nights and flattened houses and firelit skies
always in our hearts and minds we know that we are here
from black and white and sky-blue blood this is our neighbourhood
and with a grace from up above we know that we are here

Nick Knibb

Aka The Archbishop, I am a poet performer and happiest on stage at a punk gig. I am proud to be Poet in Residence at Coventry Music Museum.

The Anxious Wait

The days and nights are long now,
it is an anxious wait.
I pause, breathe in, count to four,
breathe out and count to eight.

I know the time is getting close
to hold you in my arms,
but now I'm feeling frightened,
my mind cannot get calm.

You're safe and warm inside me,
we snuggle up in bed,
the strange confusing world out here
keeps filling me with dread.

Out here we're all imprisoned,
our human rights are stripped.
A deadly virus shakes the earth,
for which we're not equipped.

I'm trying to relax enough to
bring you to this world –
your little body resting there,
head down, bum up, back curled.

Your movements are so strong now,
your kicks have so much might,
I know you're ready to come out,
I must not feel this fright.

It's 6am, I step outside,
as sun begins to rise,
the birds are singing as dawn breaks,
you stretch at my insides.

I reconnect myself with earth,
the one thing that is true,
I fill my lungs with golden light
and send it down to you.

The air is cool, a gentle breeze
now skims across my face,
this natural world, the only thing
that's filling me with grace.

I want you here beside me now,
time is moving slow,
I'm longing for you in my arms,
but can't seem to let go.

I try to calm my mind again,
it is an anxious wait,
I pause, breathe in, count to four,
breathe out and count to eight.

Chloe Morgan

I'm an art blogger, social media marketing consultant and mum of three young boys, and wrote this poem at the end of a prolonged, exhausting labour during the peak of the pandemic, right at the beginning of lockdown. Although I'm new to poetry, I found the process incredibly cathartic, and went on to safely deliver my baby boy later that day. I've been dabbling in poetry ever since, and it's helping me to navigate chaotic periods of motherhood during these very bizarre times.

Life in the time of Covid-19

Don't do, might do
can't do, maybe
what's the news
on the virus lately?

Don't know, might know
let's consult SAGE
in our new Covid-19 age

Let's take the path of least resistance
maintain two metre social distance

Embrace the new normality
of internet virtuality

Us Britons all must get a grip
using our stiff upper lip

Of course, we yearn
for the old 'normal'
when social rules
were much less formal

Our fortitude will keep us sane
until we can all meet again

All the world must now endure
until Covid-19 is no more
or Scientists find a vaccination

and we can once more go on vacation

This too shall pass
until then I will be
getting my tan on
in Coventry.

Caroline Davies

I was born in Coventry and have lived here all my life, and I'm passionate about writing. I am a member of one of Coventry's creative writing groups and have a particular interest in poetry and short stories.

Survivor

The Covid-19 survivor
is human first.
Can forgive,
is always hopeful of the future,
does not hold in the horror of the lockdown
and survives to tell their story.

Much more to the heart,
for this scar will always leave its mark,
this scar of hate,
this scar of faith.
A lockdown to save –
I live to tell this story.

No food,
no drink…
I feel my life shrink.
Hiding and waiting
until this misery ends.
Never again.

Allana Keza, age 13

Quarantine has allowed me more time for hobbies like exercise and playing guitar. The one person who has kept me sane during lockdown has been my sister – I'm lucky to have her!

Light Fingered

The back garden no longer resembled a jungle – Dad had even renovated that old greenhouse. Throughout lockdown, the children had nurtured the plants given to them by old Mrs Jackson next door, discovering their green fingers. Even their sunflowers won the village competition, and today their front lawn sale was going well.

'Dad! We've raised four pounds for the NHS already!'
'Well done, kids!'

After lunch they ran outside again, to find their roadside stall stripped of tomatoes and the ice cream tub cash box empty.

Amy Clennell

I have Cerebral Palsy and am a wheelchair user, and am partially sighted. I have a BA (hons) in Theatre and Professional Practice but have a passion for both reading and writing, although I am unable physically to do either – I listen to the spoken word and dictate whatever I want or need to write.

Disconnected

The virus presented itself during a tumultuous period of my existence. Having previously resigned from my place of work, I set up residence in a fresh city with few acquaintances. I suspected that this year was going to be yet another rocky period of 'finding myself', and set my mind to carving out a fresh start in the West Midlands.

Even before there was widely acknowledged to be a global pandemic, I already felt that everything had altered. A profound feeling of transition and hesitant optimism fettered my surroundings, despite the creeping dread of watching the virus become increasingly prevalent as time progressed.

Lockdown began, and I became more detached from the outside world. I had the promise of a new career in September, and was subsisting on my paltry savings for the duration of the confinement. I was destined to attend to my studies and amuse myself before then, and strove to make myself useful. I scrubbed skirting boards, plucked weeds from cracked slabs and slept for many hours at irregular intervals. Little studying was accomplished, and academic procrastination became my best friend once more.

A respective hermit by nature, the isolation initially appeared to be a pleasantly safe and comfortable vacuum. Existing in a universe consisting of brick wall and anxiety ridden trips to corner stores was not unfamiliar, and I settled into quarantine life quite promisingly. Existential grievances have been common haunts in my brain for decades, and now my worries and fears felt as though they had ample justification for the first time. Crossing the road to avoid pedestrians became normal, and my dislike of eye contact and small talk with strangers no longer felt hostile or unusual.

Many cups of tea were consumed, and many books devoured. Despite my isolation, empathy for others pervaded my senses. Teary contemplations became solemn evening rituals. Weeks merged together, and a pre-existing fault with memory recall intensified as my routine disintegrated.

Without a job, my sense of self-worth was at risk of teetering closer to the murky abyss. I had to rediscover a personal motivation to perform tasks unrelated to workplace advancement. I still can't cook or play the piano, but I have memorised the dialogue in my favourite sitcoms, and I think that's something to be proud of!

As black as the day may have felt at times, calm sunshine rose in the May sky. I slapped on factor 50 for fear of reddening my chalky exterior, and sat in my tiny square yard listening to songs from the Eighties. Amidst the sound of chirping birds and middle aged neighbours settling into various attempts at DIY, The Cure sang into my ears and breathed a sense of calm into my mind.

As disconnected as we can feel in this time, the suffering and hard work of so many people has awakened a sense of goodness, care and community within our nation, and indeed globally. Whilst political issues continue to unravel before our confounded eyes, certain discrepancies and ambiguities appear trivial in comparison to the fragility of life, good health and existence.

Yes, we are living in strange times. Life is strange, and has been strange for millennia. We can only hope to regain our confidence and learn to care for each other more when emerging from this sombre experience. We should remember to value the hard work and kindness of people from a variety of backgrounds who deserve much more than a round of applause, and look after those who are more vulnerable than ourselves regardless of whether there is a public call of urgency to do so.

Grace Connoley

I'm currently studying to be an English teacher at a school in Coventry so most of my time is spent reading and learning. My favourite bands are The Cure and Alice in Chains, and I'm looking forward to attending some local shows once lockdown eases!

A Tin of Italian Peeled Plum Tomatoes

It was like sitting in the chapel at the crematorium. The service and the platitudes were over; the wooden box, carefully varnished reflecting the dull light and the occupant's favourite song being played so quietly that the mourners strain to listen, then the electric motor that drives the conveyor cuts in and the coffin slides away. Forever.

And that's what it felt like – normal life, drifting away, and the tears well up in the throat and people want to shout, 'Stop, bring it back, he's changed his mind, he doesn't want to go any more.'

There it is, the announcement. We were all expecting it, but, like a terminally ill relative who we know was near to death, it still took us all by surprise.

Jack watched the television from his bed in the living room; the lads came round and moved it down last autumn when the stairs got a bit too much. The four girls took turns to come and help Jennifer with the housework and always brought two or three grandchildren to muck it up again afterwards. Elaine was there on that Monday, with her two youngest; Mary would do Wednesday. They didn't have a rota, that would make it seem like a chore and it wasn't.

Jack wasn't famous, never made the Z list let alone the B list, the nearest he got to celebrity status was when he won the knobbly knees competition at Butlins in 1963 but we loved him, his family loved him. Jennifer loved him through thick and thin, and there were times when it was very thin, times when he cycled down to the Coventry market to look for bits of scrap wood to burn on the fire; the time he ran all the way home on a Thursday afternoon with his unopened wage packet and stuck it in the bailiff's hand with seconds left before the sledgehammer took the front door off. They had a tin of peeled plum tomatoes in the cupboard and no money. That's what two weeks on the box* did back then, in sickness and in health, but you only got a wage for health.

The neighbours in that little row of houses off the Foleshill Road did their bit. Raymond, two doors down, kept chickens and gave them a couple of eggs; the lady in a sari at the corner shop sliced off two rashers of bacon and forgot to put it on the tab; someone gave them half a loaf and cut them off a piece of Stork Margarine, still in its greaseproof wrapping.

That's how it started really, the Thursday evening ritual, two rashers of fried bacon, crispy, along with at least one runny fried egg and a tin of Italian Peeled Plum Tomatoes. A runny yolk provided the necessary colour, the vortex of red yellow and orange as the yolk and tomato juices swirled together on the plate. When the kids were all at home Jennifer would butter two whole loaves and hands would leap out from every corner of the table grabbing the bread and scraping torn pieces into the batik colours of the plate. This is haute cuisine on a Thursday night, sitting in front of the telly – food, with a mug of hot tea.

Jennifer knew, the kids all knew, Jack was not upset about it, he tried to make light of it. 'Get me a book – not too long, I want to finish it.' The lads would laugh but the girls didn't find it so funny. Jack would laugh and the laugh would become a cough and Jennifer would have to help him put the nebuliser on and he would sit in his upright chair and wheeze until he could get his breath.

The first week was a novelty until Sandra came round wearing a face mask to bring the groceries. She had to leave them on the step and take a couple of paces back. 'Sorry Mam, not everything you asked for, they're queuing outside of Morrisons, there's no eggs and no tinned stuff, people are fighting over a tin of baked beans...'

'No tomatoes.' Jennifer emptied the carrier bag onto the table. 'No tomatoes and no eggs – what's going to happen on Thursday?'

It's never the big things. The stock market fell a hundred points, the dead were statistics instead of names, but all that was on the television, not in Eastern Green.

'We can't have a Thursday without tomatoes!'

Jack didn't make Thursday.

He didn't get the virus, he just slipped away; it was expected. Jennifer phoned them all in turn, all six, starting with John, the eldest and working down to Sandra. 'It's the little things that keep you sane,' she said.

They took Jack away the same morning. Only Jennifer got to see the relaxed smile on his face, calm and easy, the whiskers greying his skin.

Only six mourners allowed at the crematorium. Jack

wasn't one for religion, but he'd made a lot of people happy in his eighty-four years. Sandra said she would stay and watch from the Phantom Coach car park, being the youngest. They argued for a while, but someone had to miss it. No wake, no big send off, all the members at the bowls club, his friends from the old Massey Ferguson assembly line... they would have filled the chapel.

When the coffin moved on its rollers Jennifer reached out as if to pull it back. Alma Cogan sang the Tennessee Waltz, tears dripped onto the wooden benches and they left before the next half dozen came in with their grief.

The cars pulled out of the gates onto Charter Avenue. Sandra stood in the sunshine along with the bowls club, the men from Massey Ferguson, Raymond and the lady in the sari, socially distanced; each reflecting the rays of the sun from the top of a tin of Italian peeled plum tomatoes.

**The box, local slang for being on sick pay.*

Joe Reynolds

I am 71 years old, married to Julie and have five daughters and nine grandchildren. I am an amateur musician (saxophone), and a keen runner, cyclist and swimmer. I worked in engineering and have an OU degree in maths. My small claim to fame is that I am the sax player on the hit single 'Three Minute Hero' by Selector.

A Coventrian's Lockdown Lament

When I was young, the only Corona
I knew was the lemonade pop –
man in a van delivered it weekly
to save my mum going to the shop.

One fateful day the man didn't turn up
'He's gone off to China,' said Len.
When he returned, he'd picked up a virus
And we never saw him again.

Now it's come back, this Coronavirus.
It's rampaging, unchecked, worldwide,
spreading panic wherever it touches –
the only cure – all stay inside.

So here I am and indoors I must stay,
marooned in self-isolation.
Struggles with word-search, crossword, sudoku
are adding to my frustration.

I sit inside here, mentally jaded,
so fed-up with TV and books.
If I step out, I become a pariah –
the victim of withering looks.

Boris allows me one weekly outing,
so I can stroll down to the shops...
but I'm mindful that any excursion
risks questions from our local cops.

Yesterday's highlight – viewed through the window –
Was seeing a car passing by.
It was a red one, driver a woman
but where was she going – and why?

Others seem perky, busy and hopeful,
with never a whinge or a frown –
I'm stuck in lockdown, bored and inactive
just letting the news get me down.

Born in this city, will I survive it –
Godiva and Sky Blues my scene?
Boffins have gloomed us – maybe they've doomed us –
by naming it COVKID-19.

Craig Campbell

Serial Killers

Forget gardening and decorating – much of my lock-down time has been spent on historical criminal research. Did you know that John Wesley Hardin killed 42 people? Ted Bundy 30? Billy The Kid 21? Fascinating.

If a couple of hundred local people happen to read this, statistically I should reach the four thoughtless Coventrians alluded to in this piece.

Firstly, Simon the Cyclist. Vanity, not exercise, was your driving-force those windy April days in the Memorial Park, as you pounded round the paths, striving to improve your time-trial averages. You shouldn't have been out with that high temperature. Not wanting to sully the wheels of your thousand-pound bike by veering onto wet grass, you wove between umpteen socially-distancing walkers and flew past several oldies, momentarily resting on benches, showering them all with invisible micro-droplets of your infected sweat. Over the weeks you were responsible for twenty-five cases and at least five deaths. I rename you Peter Sutcliffe.

Next, Belligerent Brian and your wife, Dithering Doris. Brian, just because the brave, previously virus-free paper-girl inadvertently dropped off a 'Sun' instead of a 'Star', there was no need to chase after the poor lass and shout in her face. Her symptoms never showed but over the next month a couple of deaths could be attributed to contaminated newspapers. And Doris, remember your sneezes in Asda as you kept picking up tin after tin, packet after packet, then returning them to the shelves after deciding, eventually, to go down the own-brand route? When a corrupted tin of beans found its way into the local care-home – carnage. You are now dubbed Fred and Rose West.

Finally, Vince the Venturer. Thought you'd got immunity after a mild dose. Had to use your bus-pass, just to see how social-distancing worked on public transport. Absolute apocalypse in Walsgrave Hospital after Nurse Nikki touched the same bus grab-handle on her way to work. Arise, Harold Shipman.

You four. Famous? Infamous even? No way. But just as deadly as any serial killers in history.

Craig Campbell

Born in Keresley Hospital in the reign of King George VI, a Cov Kid but with deep Scottish roots, living in Cheylesmore for all but eleven years in exile in Chapelfields. King Henry's educated, then a Business Studies degree at what is now Cov Uni. Fifteen years crawling up a lucrative but boring corporate ladder to nowhere before switching to primary school teaching for eleven years, then as a supply teacher until early retirement in 2013. Since then a life of leisure interspersed with writing short stories and poetry. That's me – Jack of all trades, master of none.

Trapped

I was trapped in a world that was not right,
there were fences stopping us from achieving,
there were silly walls and stupid rules...
I was trapped.

I was trapped in a TV,
I was trapped in a cage,
I was trapped in my own mind with no way of escaping...
I was trapped.

I was stuck behind bars with a maximum space for movement,
I was stopped from reaching my potential,
The road was always uphill...
I was trapped.

I was in a boxing match,
my opponent was four times my size,
I had no chance,
I was trapped.

Life is the sea – sometimes it's rough, sometimes it's calm,
life is the news – sometimes it's good, sometimes it's bad,
life is a prison...
I was trapped.

There was a virus,
we were in lockdown,
I was trapped...

I was trapped.

Ella Wilkinson, age 12

I live with my mum and dad and my two older brothers. I like dance and I absolutely love athletics – I go to an athletics training club. I have a dream to be in the Olympics when I'm older – I have had this dream since I was very young.

Not Too Bad

My lockdown is boring,
my lockdown is sad,
but most of all,
my lockdown is bad.

Not being able to talk to my friends,
snacking from daybreak until the day ends,
making use of cardboard and plastic
making signs to help our NHS.

Always making use of tricks in science,
like a potassium permanganate grenade,
using its combustion
to expand and explode all over the place.

So I guess it's not all boring,
it could be funny,
it could be sad…
but most of all…
it's not too bad.

Aiden Ahearn, age 12

I like sport and exercise and I also read. My main interest is engineering, and I like to dismantle things and put them back together. I'd say I can be a bit hyper at times, but I'm also kind.

One Thing After Another

Jo Johnson stood at her bedroom window gazing out at the scene below. There was not a lot to see. If it were not for the comings and goings next door, the street would have been deserted like so many Coventry streets, as in other cities, other countries, other continents. A world in lockdown – her world, in the grip of a global pandemic.

Just a few short weeks ago everyone was busying themselves with their daily lives and then suddenly, unexpectedly, a new virus had emerged and everything changed. Life was put on hold.

Jo looked upwards; the sky was a beautiful blue, the sun shining brilliantly. After six months of relentless rain, the sun had finally appeared from behind a dark, murky cloud just as the Prime Minister announced that everyone except key workers must stay home. It was almost as if it had been waiting for this precise moment.

As a septuagenarian, Jo was included in the first group of people advised to stay at home for four weeks. It seemed ludicrous. Four weeks! Were they serious? She was not staying at home for four weeks for anyone! Yet less than a week later, she was in self-isolation, terrified of going out the front door, gripped by fear of the unknown. And the more she learned of this new virus, the more her fear grew – fear of infection, fear of passing it on. Even an essential shopping trip became an ordeal, causing her heart rate to accelerate the moment she stepped into the street, and taking some time to return to its normal state after her return home.

She found it difficult to comprehend the sheer magnitude of the situation. The virus had begun in China towards the end of last year... but that was China. Thousands of miles away. It wasn't going to affect her. It wasn't going to get this far. At least, that was what she had thought. And then suddenly it was in Italy and Germany and rapidly sweeping across Europe, crossing borders and seas until it reached British shores. Covid-19; mean, aggressive, intent on destroying humanity. Life had changed dramatically.

Jo picked up a book, tried to read, but she could not concentrate. She had difficulty concentrating on anything these days, and not just because of the virus.

She thought about the peaceful existence she used to enjoy. She liked spending time home alone, reading, writing, contemplating, but she also liked her freedom, the freedom of choice, the ability to shop wherever and whenever she wished, to visit family or friends, to take advantage of opportunities being offered in the community. She attended music and dance sessions, sang in two choirs and collected her young grandchildren from school twice a week. Then in early January the builders moved in next door, stripped the property down to a bare shell and began a complete rebuild of the inside. Her peaceful existence was no more.

Jo looked towards the window where the sun was flooding in. Why couldn't it have been like this back then? It had rained – every day, sometimes all day. She had been really thankful for her daytime activities which had provided an escape from the persistent drilling, hammering and banging which by now felt as though it was going on in her head as well as on the other side of the wall. Pounding, pounding, pounding.

Then came lockdown and, right on cue, the sunshine. Although by then she had resigned herself to spending most of her time inside, the mere fact that she was no longer at liberty to leave as and when she pleased seemed to amplify the incessant noise from next door tenfold. Even the garden, with the inviting warmth and brightness of the sun, provided no tranquillity.

It was virtually impossible to find a room in which to sit where she would not be disturbed by the builders. She was spending increasing amounts of time with her hands clasped around her head, silently cursing them. And sometimes, not so silently.

The building work continued. The house shook. Jo's head pounded. She remained inside, tearing her hair out. No visits to or from family or friends. No hugs from the grandchildren – how she missed them. And how she hated that noise from next door, pounding, pounding, pounding.

Jo exchanged emails with friends and maintained telephone contact with her daughter who introduced her to video calling. What an amazing invention… once you got the hang of it. She could watch her granddaughters, see their beautiful smiles, their infectious laughter, their more serious faces as they settled down to read her a story before they went to bed. Then they watched as Jo read to them, until something else grabbed their attention and they were off. She would watch their antics until they returned to the camera, pulling faces and talking in silly voices, and it reminded her just how much she was missing them. She wondered how long this situation could go on. As good as video calling was, it was no substitute for the real thing.

The days came and went, and so did the builders. Banging, drilling, pounding, pounding. Sometimes Jo thought her head might explode. She began to fear for her sanity. She kept asking herself if things would ever be normal again. And she kept telling herself that of course they would.

There is always hope.

Irene Wright

I am a retired clerical assistant, having lived and worked in Coventry all my life. I have two sons, a daughter and two granddaughters. My hobbies and interests include reading, writing, dancing, singing and making music.

A Virus With More Manners

A virus with more manners would have waited 'til at least
Oktoberfest, SPOTY, or Time's Person of the Year shortlist.
But Covid-19, protein coat and those all-round, all-weather
spikes on, early doors, was not in waiting mood.

And in theory, time was on its side. Time – and opportunity.
A Dettol-touting president, and those sunny April must-haves:
all-round-to-ours barbecues, sunbathing-in-parks-as-exercise,
and bread a pound cheaper a hundred miles away.

But then the silence fell. And the world, time on its hands, stood
back a couple of metres. Frenzied rhythms slowed; opportunity
(never one to miss an opportunity) kicked coronavirus
firmly in the lipid membranes 'til it was down.

And we clapped the heroes of our clapped-out NHS, Thursdays, eight
on the dot; biked back through time – traffic like 1955; Zoomed
slowly like we'd never Zoomed before (which, mostly, we hadn't). And
lived those dragging days and helter-skelter weeks.

Jeremy Bevan

I am 59, and a civil servant who is privileged to be able to do a lot of writing for a living. A keen cyclist and volunteer with Coventry community newspaper ECHO, I have lived in Coventry for over 35 years. In 2020 I began training to become an ordained minister in the Church of England.

Just Like a Sunday

Listen! The sound of the birds, lots of them in my garden. Living in a road used as a rat run for workers, the change now people are working from home and stopping in. It seems like a Sunday, so quiet. The empty buses still go by. Mornings are different, later and later still in my dressing gown, drinking tea. You lose your motivation to do anything except raid the fridge and watch TV or listen to the radio.

Luckily, I have my hobby of gardening. I had to sow seed, weed, water, and rearrange plants for the start of the gardening season or I would have lazed my days away! Reading is also a pleasure – I learnt a bit more technology using the ipad. Everybody needs a routine, not just children home schooling online. It's the things you miss, swimming at the local baths being one of them. Lots of cleaning and disinfecting surfaces – don't forget the wheelie bins and letter box! For something to do, try decorating your home and clearing out every cupboard!

Venture to the shops. Social distancing means no more shopping in a hurry – people speak to one another while queueing. Eerie, shops being closed. The pubs and clubs are shut so no more Saturday nights out – miss the music. Celebrations are postponed to next year, holidays are cancelled till who knows when. A lot of people losing money because they can't work. Keeping occupied is vital for your mental health, we are not moving much so lots of weight gain!

The good thing is life is less stressful, more relaxed. We have all had to adapt to not seeing our friends and family. We miss people. We have lots of time. Just like a Sunday.

Jenny Hunter

I am a widow, I'm retired, and live with a very large black cat called Oscar Wilde. He likes to put himself in front of my ipad when he wants attention, and definitely rules! He's a rescue cat and good company.

Reality

Silence in the streets
scared to venture outside
death tolls rising daily...
the past now seems so hazy.
Nowhere to be,
nowhere to see,
is this reality?

No friends to laugh with
who we now miss the most,
no distant loved ones,
unable to hold close.
Reliant on Facetime,
parties on Zoom...
Is this the future,
or is this just doom?
Nobody to meet up with,
nobody to see...
is this reality?
It's lockdown life, for me.

Lolita Tomschey-Carter, age 13

A Glimmer of Hope

All we need is a little bit of light
to help us get through these unprecedented times.
Checking the news every day,
trying to see things a different way...
loved ones lost, families grieving,
these eased restrictions seem deceiving.
But I know a way for us to cope,
and that's to keep a glimmer of hope.

Death tolls rising,
resources declining,
everyone speaks of an alleged 'peak' –
but maybe it's something more we seek?
Nonetheless, I'll keep my head up and cope,
for I have a small, bright glimmer of hope.

After all this time of being apart,
we can now see those who are close to our heart.
Even if only through a mask or phone,
it beats the bitterness of being alone.
Everyone, stay strong, continue to cope –
and hold onto your growing glimmer of hope.

Waiting for them to announce on the news,
the day there'll be an end to our blues
and when it comes, we can look back,
on the memories we've made, they will not lack.
Remember this time, when united we stood,
to beat the virus that roamed every neighbourhood.

Still together we stand, and we are no joke –
all this time kept alive by a glimmer of hope.

Lolita Tomschey-Carter, age 13

I love creative writing and poetry, it's a great form of escapism, especially during lockdown. I play guitar. I'd love to use my English or writing skills in a future career.

Positive Boredom

No school to go to –
just a local park's pretty scenery to occupy us.
No friends to talk to –
just lush green fields to help us reflect on our lives.
No playground or soft play to play in –
just flowing rivers to keep us calm.
No restaurants to eat in –
just tasty homemade food to eat.
No rushing sound of cars –
just the sweet, soothing chirp from the robins.
But spending time with our family
and getting to know our neighbourhood
is what makes lockdown special.

Nathaniel Rogers, age 9

I live with my mum, dad and little brother, and I really enjoy coding because it is fun to tell a computer how to make a game or a website. Reading is one of my favourite activities because it is infinitely imaginative and enjoyable and there is no limit to what can happen in books! When I grow up I would like to be a software engineer.

The Visitor

Since the lockdown began I'd had no visitors… until now. Up until today, it'd just been me and my old cat, Ziggy. Now, we were graced with a visitor.

Having settled the visitor, I wandered into the kitchen to make tea. Pour the water into the kettle, boil the water, warm the pot, reboil the water and make the tea. Whilst the tea is mashing, add milk and sugar to the cup. Ah, biscuits! Yes, I've got a few custard creams. I put them on a plate, nicely arranged: my visitor mustn't think I've let myself go.

I put the cup of tea and plate of biscuits on a tray and strode purposefully back into the living room. The sight that met my eyes was dreadful.

'Oh, Ziggy… whatever have you done? You've eaten our visitor! No more flies will ever come and see us, now. You naughty cat!'

Mark Rewhorn

I'm Coventry born and bred, and though now retired I've had a variety of jobs from apprentice aircraft electrician to laboratory manager. I currently live with a rescued Belgian Malinois dog and an extremely bossy cat that I know absolutely nothing about…

Locked Down

Locked down,
with no place to go,
weeks passing,
passing too slow.
People panic buying,
they were scared...
that shops would close,
they'd be unprepared.
The world seemed such
a scary place,
the virus spreading
at such a fast pace.
Childcare and work,
trying to do it all...
child in the background
of every conference call.
Emotions up and down,
some days were tough.
Not seeing grandparents,
it's been long enough.
How could meeting up be so wrong?
But we had to stay safe
we had to stay strong.
Group chats and virtual hugs
helped get us through...
cream teas and pub quizzes
also helped too.
Garden days,
long walks in the sun...

locked down in spring
but summer's begun.
Rainbows in windows,
clapping out the door...
people coming together
like never before.
NHS staff worked so hard,
deserved their clap and cheer.
People lost their lives in 2020,
the Covid-19 year.

Sophie Kelly

I live with my husband Joe, son Rowan and dog Rupert, and work for a distance learning university based in Coventry. I have always enjoyed writing poetry and during the lockdown had more time to reflect and write. I'm turning thirty later in the summer and looking forward to celebrating my milestone birthday.

Dogs and Jogs

Everyone suddenly has dogs
taken to biking or jogging
the scene outside my window
never an empty street.
Lockdown rules are stretched
pass through windows
daily baked
Covid
bread.

Rob Goalby

Supermarket

Abhorrent looks toward my face mask
I feel like I'm the one who's wrong.
Queues outside are wide apart,
inside a free for all,
what use are arrows?
Can't people see?
They keep us
Covid
free.

Rob Goalby

I have worked all over the country, but Coventry has always been home – and unemployment during lockdown has provided the time to start writing again. The Covid nonets above were inspired by a desire to express the difficulties people have faced trying to adhere to lockdown rules whilst maintaining a semblance of normal life.

Perfect Day

Groaning resonated throughout the place,
I awakened in despair
my dog was licking around my face...
life just wasn't fair.

Moments later I got to my feet,
an abundance of time to spare.
I spoke to my dog about feeling defeat –
he simply did not care.

More time passed, pancakes were made,
placed my plate upon the chair –
pancakes gone, I was betrayed –
my dog just wouldn't dare!

I begged for the virus to be cured,
my dog hid in his lair...
I nearly forgot that I was bored,
I wished I was elsewhere.

Reece O' Regan, age 14

I live with my parents and older brother – my older sister has moved out now. I love art and science and aspire to become some sort of architect or engineer when I'm older. At the moment, my hobbies include swimming and drawing. The poem was inspired by my dog, Bear.

When Will Life be Back to Normal?

'When will life be back to normal?'
the sophisticated students laugh and sigh,
as the school gates close and the Year 12s cry.
Hundreds of people sick and dying,
their loved ones in sorrow and agony, crying.

The world is fighting an invisible man...
just one wrong step taken could unveil the plan.
The whole world is being put on hold
for the mask behind the enemy yet to unfold.
Isolated and desolate people all over the land
yet unity and justice still move hand in hand.

Uncertainty and loss of sight lies in the air,
as another pandemic of racism begins to flare.
Protestors fighting for equality –
yet some have led to a blind morality.
'Oh, when will life be back to normal?'

NHS workers fight day and night,
yet the marks on their faces show courage and might.
Rainbows are their sign of hope
as they carry the light back to the rope.

The pandemic has bought us a new time, new season
but the death of George Floyd was done without reason.
Mistakes have been made and lessons have been learnt
is it now time to take back all we've earnt?

The light at the end of the tunnel seems near,
yet it's so far away, and we're all still in fear.
I spoke to my friend, online, very formal...
'Oh, when will life be back to normal?'

Munotida Rabvukwa, age 12

I'm a student at Bishop Ullathorne school, I love to play netball and in the future I would love to be either a dentist or a doctor!

Lockdown Living

Lockdown living,
full of misgivings
but this prison
is actually
a prism.
The light of life is still there,
it's just refracted,
bent and deviated
like the plans we'd created.

Although dispersed,
and coerced
into isolation
and separation,
it could be worse.

Although unprecedented,
time has stood still,
not ended.
This is our chance to stop the clock
and work out what we really want.

What makes you tick?
Which bone to pick?
You've been prescribed
the time
to scratch that itch.
So do it.

I know the power of creativity
in leading you out of negativity.
This new reality
has an impact emotionally…
but there are ways of coping.

For me,
it's writing,
or poetry,
which allow my heart and head to breathe.

It teases out the unease
and untangles the web of anxiety
which has a tendency
to weave
itself into a tapestry.

I implore
you to explore
this side of yourself more.
It could unlock the door
to a fulfilment you've never felt before.
It inspired me to help create
the Sitting Rooms of Culture.

Now I'm not ignorant
of the fact
that all the problems we have
are unlikely to be solved
just by sharing art on social media.

However,
it has the potential
to be so much more than that.
It has quickly grown
into a cultural home,
a creative zone
for sharing skills and homegrown
talent in celebration.

The most beautiful distraction
from the deadly inaction
of those ruling our nation.
which has left me,
along with my colleagues,
with inadequate protection.

It's helped to drown out the white noise
of Bozza and his boys,
and despite them spouting
the same robotic rhetoric,
the only thing they're testing
is our patience
rather than our patients.

Despite the risks,
we carry on regardless.
As a nurse
I've seen the worst.
I haven't done ITU
but I've experienced enough end of life care
to see me through.

It's duty,
rather than bravery.
A role that was made for me,
and newfound campaigner
of creativity
for a positive mentality.

Lockdown living –
the age of humanity.

Kirsty Brewerton

I am a nurse who recently returned to work after a long bout of sickness. My time off gave me a chance to explore my creative side, and I found a passion for writing and poetry. I am mum to a glorious bundle of fun, my three year-old son.

Bye Bye for Now

Everyone stay
inside they say,
so what else to do
but play?

Apart from when we have to take
food to those forced to remain
inside due to their
vulnerable status.

I miss my Nana,
Grandma and grandads.
Life has flipped upside down,
like my sunglasses.

All I can say,
is have a nice day
and bye bye
for now.

Jude Powell, age 3, (with help from his mum)
Jude is a huge Thomas the Tank fan, you'll usually find him making up adventures with his trains somewhere. He's got a cheeky side and likes to play pranks and make jokes – it's rare to see him without a smile.

From the Shielded

As the chattering classes get bored linking remotely to the news channels,
the webcams not doing them any favours, with the studio lights out of
their reach...
take it from the shielded,
asphyxiation ain't fun, ain't a lark.
Not a walk in the park, two metres apart.

Household groups collide round blind corners on the way to exercise
their rights,
while right-wing pundits talk of the cure being worse than the disease.
Take it from the shielded –
civil liberties are no use to the dead,
so don't take liberties.
Find some resilience inside instead.

Not three weeks in and already they want out –
the national effort, the Dunkirk spirit, somehow now
in doubt.
Take it from the shielded –
'It's the economy, stupid,' is far from the right chant.
These people have never lived restricted,
but yet they still selfishly rant.

Is it a complex picture, or the fact that these people have never heard
'No?'
Ensured national income could be the way to go.
Take it from the shielded, restricted all our lives...

the rich must get poorer, or we'll pay the ultimate price.
You are not a martyr for staying at home,
only the NHS heroes know real sacrifice.

Andrew Bogle

I'm a writer in my late thirties. I came to Coventry as a student, and like many people, found it hard to escape its draw. I have been shielding through this period, as I am severely disabled, and this experience has heavily influenced my poetry during these strange days of isolation.

Lockdown Trio

The springtime lockdown
remote waiting and watching
garden joy and light

Women cope, no choice
resilient as the weeks pass
all women endure

It lifts cautiously
we emerge thinking forward
to the newly learnt

Faye Pettitt

I have lived in Coventry for five years with my husband and I work on a project within the local women's sector called Coventry Women's Partnership. The first poem was written in late March – I was grateful for my garden at such a strange time. The second was inspired by my work with women with multiple complex needs, how Covid-19 has further challenged their lived experiences and how, ultimately, they are strong and amazing women. The third was written as measures started to lift.

Thoughts from Covid-19

The world's a mess and I feel sick.
It's been months, we're not handling it.
Everyday people at each other's necks,
resources are stretched at the NHS,
people cut off from seeing family,
social media is getting more ugly,
uncertainty leaves black tar on fun,
high in the sky taunts a summer sun.
The world is spinning,
big business winning,
making blood money off people's grief,
it's beyond belief.
Terrified of an invisible villain,
while murderers get set free from prison.
The great British public soldier on,
doing puzzles, exercising, baking scones,
anything to put on a positive spin,
knowing in our hearts that we're trapped within
a living nightmare,
long for a time where
this all seems like a distant memory.
Looking for a remedy
but the events of these days will leave a scar,
as the world finally sees who we really are.
The death toll weighing heavy on our consciences,
what could we have done to avoid all this?
Friendships are ending, marriages shattered,
people have lost sight of what really matters.
Persecute others for not learning a skill,

they're busy battling with feeling ill!
No well wishes if you're not coughing,
it's not the only way to end up in a coffin.
I've sat here feeling very alone
battling the cloud as it begins to grow.
'You're not worth the effort, though.
You're not the one people want to know –
it'll all be over and what will you have to show?
Focused all your energy on where we won't get to go.
Want to reach out,
want to scream and shout,
please don't go out,
put on your mask, tie it in place –
how do we like the look of this brave face?

Alice Di Trolio

I am a self-published author of two poetry anthologies – ***Short Steps and Deep Breaths*** *and* ***Dark Thoughts and Happy Endings****. I hold a degree in Theology and Religious Studies from the University of Roehampton and am a member of the LGBT community, a geek with a passion for all things pop culture and a real ale lover. @aliceditrolio online.*

My Narrow Life

My garden is my haven now.
The cat is harassing the birds…
I choose my words
carefully.
Her brain is small, you see.
'LEAVE THE BIRDS!!
understand???'
She looks at me.
Does she
comprehend
my feeling about the wrens
(which she slaughtered the back end
of gawd knows when?)
'Oi!!!!'
'Oi!!!!'
She's at it again!
Watching the blue tits
pecking the nuts,
and taking a seed to a higher branch.
They know she's there.
I know she's there.
We watch each other,
the birds and I and the cat.
It's where we're at.

Mel Beech

I've always enjoyed writing poetry and never know when inspiration will hit – my family, friends and assorted jobs have all been inspirations in the past. I read about the Couch Potato Challenge while sitting in the garden and thought, 'My garden is my haven now…' The rest just poured out!

Lockdown

Covid-19 Lockdown:
*You cannot visit friends
*You cannot go outside as much
*You can go outside for one exercise a day only
*I feel alright, and OK.

The activities I can do on my settee
are play video games and watch TV.

A prism like a prison,
life is still here, just dull.
We are trapped, with a little bit of light.

There's power within us all, not being used.
We all feel sad and isolated, we want to stop the clock,
but it's too late... we have to wait.

Andrew Barr
Student at Cardinal Newman School.

The Virus and Us

Coronavirus
aka Covid-19,
a mugger, as Boris says.

There are a lot of words being used at the moment
The government's favourite one – unprecedented.
Scary.
Distressing.
Never seen before.
And, of course, lockdown...
a rather negative experience,
a waste of time.

Lockdown... it has to be
the most annoying thing in the world.
Not being able to go outside,
see your friends,
go shopping, or out to eat.
There's no Nandos or McDonalds...
how will we all cope?

Netflix
YouTube
food
TV and movies, obviously.

But...
what about new skills?
Maybe write a story,

a poem,
a song.
Enter an online competition,
try a new way to exercise,
read a book.

Together let's change our perception of lockdown,
make it worthwhile...
a valuable, memorable time in our lives
when we did so much,
discovered something new,
developed ourselves.
When we did our bit by staying inside
when our NHS were finally appreciated
for all they have done for us.

Coronavirus –
a time that made a difference
we shall never forget.

Aimee Grace Morley, age 16

I will soon be starting A levels, and my passions are media, journalism and poetry – a career in TV, radio or print journalism is my dream. I currently have a radio show, Aimee's Afternoon, on Hillz FM and write for their website, as well as working with various charity groups in Coventry.

Lock Tight

You notice how the weather changes
when you're locked down,
if very hot our balcony can also be ....
when rain skates down you're inside,
doing all those things you thought you
had done, or thought you'd done.
You heard of Les who's redecorated
half his house... he works so fast,
knows every nook and cranny.
And you think, I don't have the paint!
Can't get to the shop to get it,
so return to the easier things,
and when the bulb blows in the lounge
and you can't get out to buy a spare,
well, it'll have to wait, won't it.
Get on with what you can.

All the films on T.V. seem old,
remember 'The Deer Hunter'?
The haunting melody played acoustically,
on guitar by Aussie John Williams
on sound-track and in Symphony Hall
reminded me of a Mormon in London digs,
whose brother was a G.I. in 'Nam.
The tune again got in my head,
I hummed it anew,
think I got it right over coffee.

Couldn't go to the bistro for chatty inspiration,
just stay here and write on Memories.
Reminds me, my ink's out, printer doesn't,
can't get to where they rest, unwanted.
Soon be snack time, couldn't read.
The morning's gone, try again later…
after lunch, another story.

Martyn Richards

I've been a writer-performer since 1950 when, aged eight, my first stories won prizes in the Coventry Standard. I have acted in Coventry, London and Birmingham and performed my poems and stories across the region, most recently at the open mic at the Treehouse, Kenilworth, and have been published in Chatterbox.

My Lockdown Life

Lockdown has given me time to explore my inner self, which is often not possible in our everyday busy lives. I can certainly feel the difference between how it was before the lockdown and the present – life is different now. I have more time to listen to the birds chirp from dawn to dusk – new guests have settled in the bird house and the end of our garden. It is joyful to see them! The chicks are now hatched and fluttering around the garden and I can't stop admiring their luscious blue and yellow velvety coats of fluff.

My mum and I have been painting on pebbles – we made a ladybug, a henna art design, a heart design, a leaf, even a picture of a beach. While I was painting, an idea popped into my head – I could paint a pebble for my friend! I painted the pebble and added an extra one for her to paint herself, placed them inside a box and decorated the box. After all that, we went to her house and placed the box on her doorstep as a small surprise.

In March, we installed a small greenhouse so we could grow flowers, fruit and vegetables. It was our first try at doing this, and we sowed tomatoes, strawberries, onions, radish, beetroot, potatoes and mint. We got soil and grow bags from the supermarket, and I spotted a bicycle planter so we picked it up along the way. Some of the herbs are ready to harvest now!

My mum's birthday was a special day – we baked a scrumdiddlyumptious chocolate cake topped with juicy strawberries and healthy walnuts, but this was not enough. I wanted to surprise her with something she would never imagine. Secretly, I cocooned in my room and wondered how to make something out of nothing. I found a cardboard box and decided to make it into a birthday box, decorated with bunting and with a miniature handmade diary inside. I also made a shark brush holder to hold my mum's make-up brushes! This scrappy birthday box put the biggest smile on my mum's face – she really did like it!

Joe Wicks got us going in the mornings. After his TV workout I feel super-energised and more positive to face the day. Friday is my favourite workout day because it is dressing up day! I dressed as Hermione Granger from Harry Potter and my friend dressed as a unicorn. Joe Wicks was dressed as an inflatable dinosaur and looked hilarious!

Lockdown has made me appreciate the smallest things, and I feel it is important now to keep our blue planet safe and to live a sustainable life. I hope the world will win over this harmful virus so we can get back to our normal lives, helping to make the earth less polluted and taking care of our ecosystem.

Surabhi Badri, age 10

I am in Year Five at Ernesford Grange Primary School and really excited to share some of my thoughts and experiences during the Covid-19 lockdown period.

CITY OF QUARANTINE 2021

(or *'The Pastymes of People'*)

The homeless will be rounded up and sent to shelters.
County Lines services running to and from the city will be suspended for the duration.
We are going into quarantine.
It will be fantastic.
Our ambition is to be inclusive.
We aim to transform.

None shall leave their domiciles to walk upon the earth.

*

A ring of roads shall swallow us whole.
Walls will be daubed with digital words.
The voices of our city will be stilled.
We will surely learn the language of birds.

This will be a fantastic achievement.

*

Everything must be fantastic now
And not prosaic.
It must be 1987.
It must be 2-Tone.
Improving things cannot mean hard work and daily diligence:
Not when quarantine means no pedestrians.

*

Our fantastic NHS –
a thing from a dream.
We're all in it together,
this storm.

Hate crimes and bullying:
Poor mental health:
Climate change:
Obesity:
Inequality:

The pastymes of the people.

*

It's time to prove we're future proof
by battening down the hatches
and putting our heads in the sand.
When you're blind is the best time to drive
to a city you can be proud of –
a place of hidden assets
where the future's close at hand.

Follow us on Instagram.

*

We are going into quarantine.
Our streets will be bare.
Our shops will all be empty,
and toilet roll scarce.

We'll be crying our eyes out.
All we love will be just there,
Just out of reach
in the public square.

But I digress.

*

We will divest.
The past is gone:
Watches, ribbons, motors –
they're done.
But we're stronger. We're fitter.
We are going into quarantine.

Please follow us on Twitter.

*

We'll have a moment of silence
then we'll bang our pans.
We commissioned this virus
and it's all going to plan –

before we shut up shop, though,
let's look to our saviours:
The centrepiece that quivers and quavers.

They're just now spotting
this disaster's authors,
how long there's been
Socialism in the water:

That's what makes the rainbows glow –
from Land's End to Llandudno,
and even from Foleshill Road
to Fargo.

*

So
we are going into quarantine –
come, take a look:
We are going into quarantine.

Please follow us on Facebook.

SJ Hirons

I live and work in Coventry. I studied at the National Academy of Writing in Birmingham and have a Diploma in Creative Writing from Birmingham City University.

A Different Turn

The sky is at the clearest
it has been for many years.
The world has come together,
shedding multi-coloured tears.
There's no discrimination,
no selectiveness at all –
no hiding in the palace
from this earthly wake-up call.
A time for no complacency,
the message from above
has told us of our weakness
and our selfish lack of love.
There is a chance for us to stay,
continuing this ride –
but only if we mirror
what's on offer deep inside.

Johnnie Hall

Borrowed Time

There's nothing wrong with me today,
I woke up in the usual way,
the kettle boiled,
the tea was poured,
the toast was spread,
the hunger cured.
The news was read,
forgotten quick,
erased from mind
with just one click.
Today there's nothing wrong with me.
Tomorrow?
What will be, will be.

Johnnie Hall

I am 55 and live in Coventry, though I am generally happier in the countryside than in the city. My favourite quote? "I hate everybody equally, I don't discriminate."

Treadmill

Stepping off the treadmill,
restoring what makes our hearts lighter...
breathing, talking, laughing, walking, growing, cooking, creating.
Being kinder,
soothing the earth and listening to the birds,
reading.
Peering strangely into the other place
where we used to live
and wondering how without this
we would see how unbalanced and harmful it was
to every person, city, country, continent, land and sea,
and resolving that we never needed the treadmill,
just our own feet feeling the grass,
the earth, the sand, the water.

Daksha Piparia

I am a freelance project manager, community arts producer and also run Foleshill Creates. I live with my husband, my daughter and twin sons. I love walking and cooking and have recently discovered a love for growing vegetables. I write poetry in secret, but I suppose that's not a secret anymore...

Hope on Fairy Wings

Where have the children gone? I've looked in all the classrooms, all through the school. Maybe I have gone to the wrong place? My head did feel a little wishy-washy this morning. I've not made that mistake before though, and I have been visiting this school for almost 35 years. Maybe I have forgotten a holiday?

Perhaps everyone is in the hall – there could be a big school meeting happening, or a show. I love watching the children sing and dance... but the hall is empty. Something isn't right. My heart feels like a leaf fluttering in the wind – this isn't a feeling I have had before. I need to speak to my supervisor.

I fly as fast as I can. As I turn the corner into the work hub, Freya, my supervisor, glides towards me. Her bright pink wings are very shiny today. I cannot remember them ever looking so beautiful and sparkling. When I tell her what has happened, her face is serious. Her voice is different too, a tone I haven't heard before. Freya speaks slightly faster than usual and seems out of breath.

'You're right, something is very wrong,' Freya tells me. 'The last time I felt this way was many years ago, when the children were sent away to the countryside. It was 1939 and I had been in my placement at Bablake School – I went to check on the children and could not find them...'

My eyes are wide.

'This is when I began to feel like you do now,' Freya

continues. 'There was a fluttering in my heart. My supervisor told me that the children had been sent away to stay safe, because the country was at war. I was told that there would be frightening times ahead for us all, but that our job was to try and keep the children's hearts as happy as possible. We were no longer being asked just to check on their teeth but on their happiness too...'

Freya pauses, her eyes clouded with memories of long ago. 'It was difficult to do that, some days, but we did our best as tooth fairies to keep up with our usual work load and also keep the children as happy as we could. Now it is YOUR turn to help the children. They have been told they have to stay at home and not go to school...'

My wings begin to get brighter all of a sudden, filling up with love. I know now that I will not be visiting children at school to check on their teeth but visiting their homes. It will be a hard but important job. My role as school tooth fairy has changed and my wings are growing to hold all the love I will need to carry out this special job. With lighter and brighter wings, I can fly higher and faster.

We all come together in the meeting hall and are assigned our groups of children – my list is Max, Birdy, Evie, Rhea, Megan, Elijah, Abby, Holly and Lucie. They are friends at school but now they're at home and not allowed to visit each other or play together. I can see this being very hard for them. Freya explains that a virus is making people very sick in the human world and only a few people are allowed to go to work or school. It is called Lockdown in the human world, but Freya calls it Safekeeping.

At the beginning of Safekeeping, the children are excited to be at home with their parents, having fun. They sleep well after fun filled days, but as time goes on this happiness begins to fade. They are missing their friends, school and family. Life for them is very different now, just as it is for us.

Urgently, we hold a new meeting to see how best to help the children, and a worker called Barney comes up with the fantastic idea to fill the children's hearts with rainbows. This could work – if we place rainbows in the hearts of the children, they will begin to draw and colour rainbow images. They will begin to hope. Our wings begin to sparkle brightly, and we know it is the right thing to do.

Our plan works well. Children begin to draw and colour rainbows, putting them in their windows. They can see each other's rainbows when they go for their daily walk. They begin to smile and wave to each other as they pass by. Happiness and hope begin to grow in their hearts again!

Another meeting is being held tonight... I wonder what fabulous ideas we will come up with next?

Corina McDevitt

I am a fifty-something mum of five amazing children and nanny to five beautiful babies. Lover of life, family, friends, sunshine, meditation and anything spiritual, happily making each day the best it can be.

The Days of Lockdown

Day one in isolation and everything is fine –
everyone is feeling sane
everyone's staying in line.

Day two in lockdown and everything's OK –
everyone is running wild
but tempers are starting to fray.

Day three in lockdown, and the weather is just perfect –
but we can't go outside
so we've started an art project.

Day four in lockdown, and we are all going mad –
although the dog is happy,
my siblings are quite sad.

Day five in lockdown, and please let it end –
I'm really bored inside
but I've made a new penfriend!

Day forty-nine in lockdown and we've eaten half the house...
all the loo rolls are gone
and my only friend's a mouse.

Daisy Taplin, age 12

I'm a student at Cardinal Newman school, and my three favourite subjects are art, drama and English. My hobbies include painting, drawing and reading.

What Can Be Done?

I didn't know a time
like this would come.
I can't even run –
Some say it's dangerous.
Some say it's madness.
What can be done?

My heart melts
every time I hear
another loved one is gone.
What can be done?

All day long we attack
the fridge…
but out there
Coronavirus is attacking
elders, adults, kids.
What can be done?

Ashpreet Dehal, age 13

I love to write poems as it helps take my mind off stuff, and I like travel too… it expands my imagination and gives me ideas for songwriting, poems and more.

Does Spaghetti Really Have an Expiry Date?

Day 17
I start in the kitchen,
take out every dented tin and sunflower patterned plate,
I ask Google if Safeway's spaghetti really has an expiry date.
I find metallic blue touch-up from two cars ago,
eight pesetas and a disc for installing Windows XP.
That night, I remove 'tinned peas' from my shopping list
and cook spag bol for dinner.
I don't know why but neither of us had stomach ache
so Google must have been right about the pasta.

Day 18
Placing ten plastic tubs on the breakfast table,
I remember Nan bringing them home –
her hands smoothing sticky labels onto their lids,
using her best biro and capital letters to write:
EARRINGS. HAIR CLIPS. NAIL VARNISH.
I recall her lining them up on my dressing table,
pointing the pen tip my way and saying:
Now don't you let it get into that state again.
I offer an apologetic shrug to the urn on the bookshelf.
The first box, NAIL POLISH, is a Homebase colour chart
of early Noughties Barbie pinks and glo-stick greens.
On opening, the contents cling to hardened bristles
and glob onto my fingernails like marmalade.
This time I don't need Google:
the next few hours are spent gently tipping polish remover
into every pot of gloop in an attempt to resuscitate them.
That night I paint each toe nail a different colour.

I don't understand why remover resurrects polish
but I do know that Nan had many useful tips.

Day 19
I take two buckets of warm bubbles to the bathroom.
The window sill has long been a museum of discarded
bottle lids and fossilised soap stains.
I turn the tap on, cold water for rinsing fizzes into the tub.
At some point I notice the black speck of a fly floating
towards the far end.
With my palm flat, I scoop it out, spread its sodden wings
apart with my fingernail and gently blow –
again, again, willing life back into its little lungs
until one tiny leg twitches. I finally breathe out,
not knowing why it's so important,
just knowing that it is.

Emilie Lauren Jones
Previously published by HCE magazine and Half Moon Books, due to be published with Under the Radar and Oneworld Publications, I was commissioned by UK City of Culture for the project 'Humans of Cov'. I am part of the Nine Arches Press 'Dynamo' scheme and poet in residence for Hillz FM. I once abseiled down Coventry Cathedral.

All This and More

Loss and disbelief and worry,
distancing socially, not emotionally.
Isolation, trepidation and fear,
sadness and anger and clapping,
fury and acceptance and change.

Helping and sharing and caring,
shopping and cleaning, tidying and doing.
Sleeping and eating, baking and reading,
gardening and walking, weeding and weeping.

Missing and hoping and moments of joy,
building connections, exploring and holding.
Receiving and just being and giving thanks,
letters and phone calls and smiles of kindness and appreciation,
tempers and silence, walking and talking.

Sunbathing, listening, cooking and zooming,
planting and growing, building and learning.
Laughing and queuing, waiting and stretching,
loving and time. All this and more,
and so much more.

Debbie Riordan

I came to Coventry in 1982 to study Social Science at the poly, and stayed. I've lived all over the city, married my teenage boyfriend, raised a family in Earlsdon and worked for Coventry City Council for over 22 years. Now I teach yoga, garden, walk our dog and look after my new grandson!

Time

Lockdown gives me time
to complete the things I love to do.
Lockdown gives me the opportunity
to practice the craft of writing poetry.
A long journey
may often entail failures, but
challenges are part of the journey;
they help you to discover
solutions to problems,
take your disappointments
and learn from them.
This will make you
a stronger person...
take one step at a time
and improve each day.
My disability has given me
plenty of challenges,
and I have fought through them.
Don't let anything
or anybody
hold you back.

Jay Joshi

Writing poetry has given me a purpose and direction in life – I sometimes struggle to articulate the spoken word in conversation, but poetry has given me a voice to express my emotions. I'd like to thank my family for all their support.

An Infectious Laugh

He is waiting in the wings,
perfecting his act,
taking his cue
to seek out the vulnerable,
observing and pursuing weakness and idiosyncrasies.

Conquering the world by storm,
his twisted, perverse humour ridicules and overpowers,
the uniform, mundane and privileged,
finding its way into the theatres and air waves,
with no pity or remorse.

Rolling in the aisles, helpless,
we fall under the spell of this ongoing, sick joke,
a relentless, dry onslaught,
as he laughs out loud,
laughs at our expense.

One more comic turn, a final push,
and he'll be laughing on the other side of his face.
To the sound of rippling applause,
the curtains are opening
and I think I am having the last laugh.

Junie-Marie Flynn

Having always been a creative person, lockdown for me has been a journey of learning, self-reliance and consideration for others.

Why, Mummy?

Why can't I go back to school, Mummy?
Why can't I see my friends?
Why can't I visit Grandma, Mummy?
When will this ever end?

You tell me there's a virus, Mummy,
but it's hard to understand.
It makes me feel so unsure, Mummy,
please will you hold my hand?

I'm feeling so angry, Mummy,
because everything has changed,
that's why when things don't go my way,
I fly into a rage.

I want to go to class, Mummy,
see my friends and play a game,
I'm just relieved that in all this mess,
you remain the same.

You still tell me when I'm naughty, Mummy,
you still take me on your knee,
you put your arms around me Mummy,
you say that you love me.

Suki Fitzgerald

I've lived in Coventry for twenty years and run a small art business, mostly selling painted stones, as well as parenting my two children. I've not written much poetry before, but lockdown has proved to be a creative time for me and I thought I'd have a go!

Lockdown Fever

It's day three billion, five hundred and something or other,
or so it feels.

Staying in one room with my family,
because that's where the WiFi is strongest.

The government says,
stay home, stay safe, protect the NHS.

They sent me a letter,
so I'm staying home for at least twelve weeks.

Three months,
ninety-one days…
can't go to the shops, or even for a daily walk.

Have to stay in my own home,
why me?

It's scary to think,
that one little virus
has caused so much grief and disruption
to our daily lives.

Even the dog is suffering
from lockdown fever,
doing loops and loops of the garden,
and round and round the house.

My phone dings again with another message.
Staying in touch with friends is so easy!
What would I do without it?
At least it's not the pandemic of 1918.

Hopefully I won't have my birthday in lockdown…
do you think it'll last till the end of September?
My brother is definitely celebrating his
without anyone else but us.

He's happy though, face glued to his PC screen,
the best self-isolator that exists.

So, for now,
we keep going with the daily routine –
up, breakfast, online school, break.
Out in the garden if the weather is nice,
stuck inside if not.

But staying safe is all that counts,
and I'm grateful we're all still OK.

Zuzanna Tams, age 12

I love animals and horse riding, and reading too. I have been shielding for the last fourteen weeks as myself and my family all have heart conditions. It'll be nice to get back to normal soon!

Making History

Covid-19 is a time of fear,
but don't worry, the NHS is here.
Wash your hands for twenty seconds,
walk for an hour but no more errands.

You may miss your family and friends,
but know their love for you never ends.
This virus is a deadly killer,
so take an online class or cook the dinner.

It has been an experience of good and bad times –
we can't break the rules, have to stay in line.
This pandemic has not been in vain,
for all the knowledge we have gained.

Covid-19 does not discriminate,
it takes all ages from cradle to grave.
We remember the lost and celebrate the saved –
we will get through the dangers we've braved.

We've learned a lot from this pandemic,
and let our imaginations grow.
Remember this will all be history,
in eighty years or so.

Aoife O'Brien, age 13

I have two younger brothers and I am a student at Cardinal Newman Catholic School in Coventry. I love to read and write and enjoy Irish dancing, swimming, sports and learning French. I play tin whistle and have twice qualified for the 'All Britain'. I enjoy travelling and love to visit my cousins in the Czech Republic and Ireland.

Summer Has Arrived

Sheltered, I am home, safe from all the harm that people experience outside. I am not concerned with my health, nor with the health of my close relatives. Having no idea what to do, I sit and stare at the empty wall hoping for something to happen... yet I do not know what. I inspect each scratch, each crack in the plaster just to focus on something other than the media outside.

Reluctantly, the pressure of my phone constantly buzzing with headlines overwhelms me, and I check my screen and see the chaos which rules the world. I watch the death count tick up slowly, as lives are taken away. Only one question is in my mind – why do I need to know all that, if all it brings to me is sadness? But I persist, searching for an answer to a question that I myself do not know.

Placing my phone onto the desk, I see the rays of the sun outside delicately touch the lush, emerald grass. What was once a boring sight has now become my only view of nature, my only source of peace, the only way in which I can escape the stress of the world.

It is at home that I am safe, but with just one view of my phone I feel like I'm on a foreign planet. On a planet millions of light years away from earth, on which no one can hear me scream.

Looking up, I see the trees slowly sway with the winds, leaves slowly brushing against the walls of buildings. Behind the trees, huge giants heave their way through the sky – clouds are tranquilly drifting through. On a day like today, the sky is a diamond blue colour near the horizon, fading as it moves up to a vivid white. High in the sky, the beautiful flaming sun is like a beacon of hope in a world ruled by plague. Taking over the room, is the ticking, the slow yet rhythmic noise that is behind me from my clock. And with each second that passes, with each blink of the eye, the world changes…

I move my attention to the people on the street, staring deep into their faces, watching their emotions shift. Some are chained down by fear, holding their hands right next to their mouths and bowing their heads down as they pass other people. Others make it seem as if this world has continued its day-to-day affairs and has not stopped during this event. They are waving and smiling to whoever they pass.

I do not know where I am on this spectrum of emotions. I feel like I am stuck in a tug-of-war battle: on one side is my mind, my common sense, my knowledge that most likely I am safe from this virus, while on the other is the media, the news, the websites that only care about me reading their articles and not about how I feel.

As I am pulled one way my emotions follow and I'm left in a focused state of survival, when in fact the world hasn't stopped and there are so many things to do, so many books to explore. Stuck in this cycle, I am left constantly thinking about this one event – about this fear in the atmosphere. I know I'm safe at home, but how am I meant to feel safe when there are hundreds of websites telling me I'm not?

I lie down, resting my head from the raging storm which

brews in my mind. In the palm of my hand I hold a book... normally, I would rest and read the book and even listen to some music. I am unable to rest my mind, though. I am forced to lie awake, my eyes open, staring at the ceiling.

I remember – not so long ago – I would have loved staying at home all day, free from the stress of the world. But now I feel as if I am locked in with all the stress at my own house, every thought of staying at home brings me one step closer to the border drawn in sand between the sane and the insane. Once again, the noise of the clock takes over the room, each tick reminding me of the lives being lost and of how insignificant my actions may be.

Closing my eyes, I am transported into a world of my imagination, a world where I can do whatever I want without feeling pain, without feeling forced to do something else I'm meant to do. And so I do the one thing that I want right now: I leave my house.

I can feel it: the rays of the sun touching my face, the breeze flowing through my hair, the noise of the birds singing in the background. I am able to leave the cell which I once called home.

In the distance, I can see my friends. They are standing, smiling and holding hands as they walk towards me. I'm relieved to see them safe at last, for the first time in a while. I see homes empty with people standing outside, children talking to one another, people playing and even a few people in front of their houses selling lemonade.

'Summer has arrived,' I whisper to myself.

Bartosz Zygowski, age 15

I was born in Poland and moved to England at a young age. Being able to speak two languages has been a useful skill – it sometimes makes it harder to communicate, but I will not let that stop my dreams of working in the design and engineering field. I enjoy writing, drawing and creating various items, everything from creative writing to product design.

Wake-up Call

With a swish of their hooded, iridescent cloaks, twelve slender beings took their places around an oval-shaped table. The discussion began.

'They are ruining the planet with climate change, loss of biodiversity and over-population,' said one.

'Agreed,' said another. 'They need a wake-up call.'

'You're wasting your time. They never learn.'

'What do you suggest?'

'Plant another virus, like we did in 1918!'

'Touch your panel if you think we should release a coronavirus.'

Twelve panels lit up – all green.

'Good. Now, where? America? Russia? China?'

'Will mankind survive?' asked one of the beings.

'Possibly not,' replied another. 'But the planet will...'

Chris Farn

I was born in Coventry... and never left! I'm married and enjoy writing, classical music, theatre, cinema, rambling and cycling. My husband and I are looking forward to cycling across Europe once again, when we finally reach the other side of the Covid-19 pandemic.

The Human Race After Covid

Equality,
to be a reality.
No discrimination,
in every nation.
Respect?
You bet.
Justice,
and of course peace.
Jobs for all –
it's everyone's right, after all.
No prison, no crime,
this world is yours and mine.
Honesty and compassion,
truth and wisdom and passion.
No hunger, no poverty,
no oppression, more liberty.
Freedom is about what we ought to do,
it's not about what we want to do.
Opportunities,
plenty of options, sharing amenities.
Happiness for all.
Caring for each other, friendliness and all.
Good attitudes for learning,
good attitudes for yearning.
No stress,
more compassion, no homeless.
No corruptions,
changes and actions.
No violence,

no wars, let's hear silence.
Let's hear the birds singing,
and feel our ears tingling.
No vanity,
a clean environment for your sanity.
All these marches during lockdown,
people will go on, although feeling let down.
Optimism and perseverance is what we need.
We all have to be responsible to succeed... indeed.
Talking about race,
there aren't many, only one, the **Human Race.**
Grace, hope and love, but the greatest is LOVE.

Alvaro Graña

I come from Peru and worked as a primary school teacher in Coventry for eleven years before having to retire on medical grounds. I work as a volunteer for the Coventry Refugee and Migrant Centre Men's Group, and for Carriers of Hope Coventry, which also supports asylum seekers and refugees.

Making Choices

After his wife died, he became a lost soul.

Ivy had been the rock he leaned on when times were bad, the one he laughed with when times were good. It was not him that had kept up with life's many technical changes such as mobile phones and computers, it was her. She was by his side for over forty years and then, without warning, she was gone. They were born the same year and that made him feel that he was vulnerable too.

For almost a year after her passing he had isolated himself from friends and family, always too busy to go down the pub with his pals or join a family gathering. Life without Ivy was unbearable. Then, out of the blue, he had discovered singing. A friend asked him to join a singing group held at the local church hall. 'Come on, James, you'll love it! It's not a big commitment, only Tuesday evenings during term time.'

'OK – I'll give it a go!'

That was the beginning of a new life without his beloved Ivy and gradually, very gradually, he began to forget the grief, loneliness and sense of isolation that he'd felt during that first year without her. Over the next three years he'd sung with people from all over the world, some of whom had become close friends. On his 70th birthday he was in Sri Lanka, celebrating with singing friends both old and new. Some he had met in Italy, Germany and France, others he had spent time with in far flung places like India, Africa and New Zealand. His birthday party had been combined with the 'last night of the holiday' party and it went on late into the night. The food was delicious, fresh, local fare and the wine flowed freely. As the party drew to a close, people raised their glasses, proposing a toast to their favourite things.

'Singing!'
'Companionship!'
'Freedom!'
'Peace!'
'Equality!'
'Meeting again next year...'

With this a roar went up. 'See you in New Orleans/ Turkey/Rome/Madrid!' James realised with growing anticipation that he had booked a place on all these singing holidays for the following year. What memories!

Now, back in his home town of Coventry, he was all alone, had been a prisoner in his own home, for the last three months. He was unable to go out because he fell into the 'at risk' group of people who could be seriously affected by Covid-19. All his singing plans had been cancelled.

First to go had been the weekend singing workshop in Devon. He'd booked the tickets well in advance to get a better deal, but now he needed a refund. He couldn't go down to the station, where he was on first name terms with the staff, because of his 'at risk' status. When he tried phoning there was only a recorded message telling him to go online at 'wwwdotthingamy-gigdotcom'. Getting his money back had proved impossible.

Everything was done online – there was nobody to actually speak to. And anyway, just how did you get online?

It was the same with his flights to New Orleans/ Turkey/ Rome and Madrid. No one to speak to, just... go online! Things went from bad to worse. After the first ten days he had run out of bread. How can you buy food if you couldn't go out? Go online. The same story, whichever way he turned. At long last he did get online, only to find that there were no available delivery slots for the next three weeks. Throughout his life he had been proudly independent, but eventually he was obliged to ask kind-hearted neighbours to shop for him.

'Please don't worry, any Columbian free-trade coffee will do,' he had assured them. But when they came back with his shopping, leaving it on the front step, 'just in case', it was ground Columbian free-trade coffee that he found. And he had no percolator.

Never before had he felt so vulnerable. Apparently, it was his immune system that put him in the 'at risk' category, but what could he do about that? Nothing. According to the reports he'd read, everyone's immune system began to deteriorate once they reached the age of forty and from then on it was downhill all the way. He felt well – and that in turn made him feel guilty. Did feeling well mean that he had Covid-19? Was he a carrier of Covid-19? Could he be tested for Covid-19?

He had never considered age to be of importance – it was just a number, after all. Surely having a positive attitude, eating well and taking regular exercise were the things that kept you motivated. But gradually, he started staying in bed rather than going for his early morning walk. Gradually, he stopped eating and began drinking. Rather than answering the phone, he let it go to 1571.

He did not have the medical symptoms of Covid-19, but the long uncontrollable tentacles of the killer pandemic were bringing back that sinking feeling of loneliness and absolute isolation that he had experienced after the loss of his beloved wife. His mind dwelt on the uncertainties. When would a vaccine be available? Could he ever fly again? When would he be able to meet up with friends and family for a meal together?

He couldn't sleep. Bad dreams woke him through the night. Living with Covid-19 was proving to be unbearable.

It was time for him to join Ivy.

Judith E Roberts

I am a retired widow who likes to sing acapella with the National Voice Network (NVW), any time, any place, anywhere!

Care

I have only ever had one goal
in my career
and that is,
and always will be,
to give care
that is felt,
seen
and remembered
with kindness,
warmth,
and a passion that shouts loud
to make a difference.
The tears of a nurse
are not seen or heard,
but kept within.
The claps and cheers
on a Thursday night
make us stand up with pride...
we do our job
wearing our hearts on our sleeves,
giving all we can.

Su Bullimore

I am a nurse in cancer care and chemotherapy, a role I am passionate about. I am a wife and mum, as well as a loving daughter, and my twin sister is also a nurse, and also published in this anthology!

Lockdown Party

I wake with gratitude in my heart. I have been blessed with another day, another year added to my time on earth, another opportunity to see the expansive blue skies, feel the warm embrace of the sun and the tickle of the cool British breeze on my skin.

As I go through my daily rituals of bathing, breakfast and morning tea, I reflect as I read the paper, headed 18th May, 2020, with headlines dominated by Coronavirus. I am amazed that I'm here to experience yet another world shattering event... will I survive it, and be a witness, like I was with World War II?

I look down from my granny flat and see some activity in the beautiful landscaped garden, my daughter and son-in-law scurrying around. The manicured lush lawn looks like a velvet carpet, framed by pink spring blossom trees. The magnolia, azaleas and rhododendrons are blooming with colour; they whisper and beckon me towards them.

I carefully walk down the meandering garden path, and the enclosed sun trap opens up to reveal banners and balloons proudly declaring the number 90. A small handful of rebellious family have come to surprise and greet me from a distance, and I drink in the smiles and love shining from their faces, and bask in it.

Warmth creeps up inside me, a feeling of gratitude, joy and excitement, as I lap up the company I've been starved of and enjoy the culinary delights on offer. I lived to see another birthday, and will sleep with peace and contentment tonight, ready to leave this earth whenever my time is up.

Milan Jagatia

Daily Walk

The narrow road started in Coventry and edged into Warwickshire, hugging the curves of the surrounding fields. The woman looked up at the powder blue skies, around her at the green and earthy fields. She smelt the freshly cut grass, the sweetness of lavender, the hot reek of manure. She was surrounded by a choir of twittering and chirping as the tiniest birds went about their business, and the cool breeze occasionally caressed her. She felt joy and peace, as all her senses were filled by nature.

Her footsteps on the path were soft and gentle, but suddenly her hair stood on end. She listened, looked about. In the distance she heard heavy footsteps approaching. She couldn't see a soul – the curves of the road acted like a dark cloak, hiding secrets. The steps got closer and closer, heavier and heavier, faster, until they were right behind her. She was startled by a deep and menacing voice.

'Lovely day for a stroll, isn't it?'

Her heart drummed faster, panic washing over her as visions of a grave end to her life flashed before her. This was an isolated and lonely road. If she screamed at the top her voice no one would hear her. She felt for her phone in her pocket, ready to use to dial 999, and also located the sharp edge of her house keys for self-defence.

In a flash, she decided on her course of action, quickly crossing the road.

'Yes, it is,' she called back. 'But please do keep two metres apart!'

Milan Jagatia

I have lived in Coventry for almost three decades with my husband, working and raising my twin daughters in the city. I enjoy yoga, meditation, walking in nature, gardening and chatting! Creative writing has been on the wish list for years, and lockdown provided an ideal opportunity to have a go.

The Rainbow Children

'Two metres away!' they said,
so I guess I'll just sneak back up to bed,
and sigh at another day ahead,
for this is the life of the rainbow children.

Waving from our windows,
to loved ones we can no longer hold.
In these tough times our true colours show...
for this is the life of the rainbow children.

Captain Tom Moore, walking his hundred lengths,
the NHS staff, working days on end,
this is a time we are family again,
and this is the life of the rainbow children.

For now, the whole world stands still,
and it's time to show how much we care...
we'll tell them how we fixed the earth together,
for we are the rainbow children.

Enya Browne, age 12

I love musical theatre and singing and my biggest dream is to become a West End actress – I also play piano and ice skate. I love writing and have a very supportive family who always encourage me!

Poor Souls

The empty feeling inside consumes me.
I'm waiting, just waiting for a friend,
but this virus has condemned me
to this feeling of nothing.

I watch the news and see death,
nothing but devastated families,
not even allowed to go to the funeral,
poor souls.

Soon it will wipe out everyone...
the city, the country, the world...
but we still sit, waiting to be let out,
us poor souls.

These grim feelings ache
as my old hand gently presses the glass,
a single tear rolls down my cheek,
us poor lonely souls.

My house in sole darkness,
like I'm not even there,
I'm just a bunch of lonely atoms,
us poor, lonely souls waiting.

I go to my front door and smile,
to collect my food,
the only joy each fortnight,
my poor lonely soul, waiting.

It started with an innocent cough.
now I have a fever, an ache…
I can't move.
Now I'm just a soul.

A soul who has waited,
who has been set free,
into God's heaven…
I shall wait no more.

Millie Shine, age 13

I love to draw and play music, but creative writing is so much fun, it gives you a chance to express yourself!

Covid-19

Covid-19,
the worst some generations have seen.
In lockdown
we are stuck in our homes,
prisoners.

We live in this world
where global warming is just being dealt with,
where cures are starting to come out,
but for Covid-19,
it is different.

Yes, research is being done,
but too many people are passing because of it,
people leaving too soon.
The social aspect of life is slowly disappearing.
What we saw as normal, is now a risk.

What we thought was normal,
is now a thing we can only look back on.
What we thought was normal,
is now a thing we can only pray for...

All due to
Covid 19.

Nashrah Khan, age 13

I am currently a student at Cardinal Newman Catholic School, and I live with my parents, who always support me with things like this. My favourite animals are cats and some of my hobbies are art, reading and sciences. I aspire to do something within science or maths when I am older.

Quarantine

When the announcement was made, I couldn't stop smiling. There would be no school! I thought nothing could get better than that... but obviously, I was wrong. As home schooling began I quickly realised that I wanted to be at school after all – I missed seeing my friends and working in a classroom where it is easier to get help with different subjects.

The days began feeling longer and longer. I was constantly bored – I just didn't know what to do with myself. As time went by, I decided to do something to show how thankful I was for the NHS, so I did a drawing of a rainbow and put it on my window. I didn't just stop there – I decided to make small rainbow pictures and post them through all of my neighbours' doors. People really needed to be cheered up and have a smile put on their face so that is what I tried to do! I made lots of visits to my grandparents and baked different things for people, and this also helped with the constant boredom.

Every morning I did Joe Wicks – I enjoyed it, but I would still rather be at school with my friends. The lesson that I dreaded most was maths. I would have prefered to have help from my teacher than having to try and work things out that I didn't know on my own.

Thankfully, my dance school decided to do online lessons and this gave me something to look forward to, as I love dancing and I got to see my teachers and friends, even if it was only online. I also started to daydream a lot more and take myself to different places in my imagination as it was something to do. It's quite nice really, as you can take yourself places like the beach and the woods!

Quarantine has helped me to not take things for granted... things like going to school and seeing my friends, even from a distance. It has helped me become more independent too, as I can't ask for help as much as I would in school. Even so, I can't wait for things to go back to normal so I can see my friends again!

Rose Hussey, age 12

I love to read and write stories, and have just started reading The Hunger Games and am loving it. I love dancing, my favourite dance is Irish. Penguins and sloths are my favourite animals, and my dream is to have a short story published, so thank you!

Solitude is an Attitude

A single space
exists amongst the masses.

Isolation has become our relation,
hidden behind walls
that have grown out of all proportion.

We are cut from a cord
but we cannot be separated…
we need oxygen.

Life found in windows
that open and let in the air
to carry on the wind
our tears and despair.

Michala Gyetvai

A Robin Flew into my Garden

A robin flew into my garden,
tilted his head in greeting.
He flew in for a meeting,
him and me,
me and him –
the only guest allowed in.

Michala Gyetvai
I am a Kenilworth-based artist working between painting, poetry and textiles. My work looks at materials, nature, the handmade, the human hand and how it shapes our existence in a digital era.

Cov Kid

I'm a Cov Kid living through the Covid,
our city is it gritty, no pity.
Loo rolls buy some, might try some Dyson
ventilators broke, die some, cry some.
I'm a Cov kid living through the Covid
man on the street with his script in his hand
couldn't care less if meeting is banned.
Spit on a nurse, you're cursed –
deserve to die, Cov kid,
wooden box, close the lid.
Is your mother proud when they say so loud,
he's a player, slayer,
how you feelin' dealing in death?

Two metre rule, not a fool
but a lonely lady and a sad granddad
needed some food, not broke but 70 plus.
You write me off cos I'm not a toff,
I can't get the test like the rich,
but I've got the cough.

End of the Wood can you reach it
Potter G and all your crew, can Lee see it
On the Hill of Tiles
need to bleach it.

Stay at home, no schools, the rules
one hour out, don't flout
shout out trying, crying, dying

back to the Grange, life rearranged.

Held me since I was first born
now mother mourns
I'm as hard as nails, mother wails
What's that you said, hell no,
Nan's dead.

YOLO, furlough, booked it but I can't go,
stay alert but we're hurt though
not working, not shirking, my mental health,
what I need is mental wealth.

Cov kid, I'm only nine, should be fine, mum's drinking wine.
Cov kid, only 19, can I beat this, what? You can't treat this.
I can't hold you, you can't hold me, don't let me die please.
Cov kid age of 90, shielded, the sword is wielded,
I fought back, now in this battleground it's friends I lack.
Say goodbye and miss you, send a kiss too…
I'm a Cov kid living through Covid.

Elaine Wallace

Born in County Coundon, drank in The Holyhead, danced in The Parrot, Parsons Nose on the way home. If you know, you know.

What will the legacy of Covid be?

Five o'clock briefing, friends not meeting,
isolating, shielding, no tactile greeting
furloughed and frightened
anxieties heightened –
is this what the legacy of Covid will be?

Queuing and queuing to get into places,
keeping a distance in two metre spaces.
Grief for those dying in solitary isolation,
leaving loved ones behind full of pain and frustration –
is this what the legacy of Covid will be?

Key workers weary, their spirits adrift,
find sad, empty shelves at the end of their shift,
paucity of pasta and a dearth of flour –
what chance of a meal at this late hour?
Is this what the legacy of Covid will be?

Yet amidst the pandemic, turmoil and confusion,
there's a strength drawn from hope, charity and communion.
The kindness of strangers and neighbours unknown,
shopping, delivering or chatting by phone –
this is what the legacy of Covid could be.

A smile from a walker and a cheery hello,
'Are you keeping OK, mind how you go!'
Dog walkers, fundraisers, sewers and bakers,
giving time freely with love and kind faces –
this is what the legacy of Covid should be.

As the dark storm of Covid begins to abate,
a rainbow with its pot of gold will await.
That pot is for all to find and to share,
a new normal of kindness, compassion and care.

This is what the legacy of Covid must be.

Janet Wilson

I have lived in Coventry all my life. I love going on holiday and exploring new places – and when not on holiday I am equally happy at home with my family and cat!

The New Norm

Dinner on my doorstep
Home cut haircut
Insomnia the new norm
Middle of the road for a walk
Two chevrons to talk
Screen time scream time
Quiet… the birds hear everything
Quiet… the birds sing everything
Dandelions and daffodils
Bluebells and blossom
Kindness and care.

Mary Courtney

The Hair

I see hair taking over the armchair, taking over the sofa, covering the kitchen cabinets, curling over the carpets, crawling up the doors, sprouting through the letterbox... tendrils and tendrils of it... growing like ravenous brambles, sprawling out, out onto the street, out onto the pavement, reaching out for the lamp post, curling round and round, winding round and round the big finger of the lamp post, tighter and tighter... until... the hair pulling tighter and tighter, it pulls the sofa out through the letter-box, pulls it out, out onto the street, out onto the pavement... scudding down with a scuffle and down with a thud, catching its breath, rearranging its cushions... turning around and fluffing the cat, fluffing the cushions, and thanking the big overgrown hair... thanking the hair, for getting him out of there.

Mary Courtney

Once went shopping for fingernails for a fish – Sponnie the mechanical fish from Spon End. Makes animations and films with other people. Brought a Wordrobe Wardrobe to a library and Art of the Micronosphere to giant digital screens. Often found in her cave drawing a poem. www.marycourtneycoventry.com

Love in Lockdown

He is with me day after day,
night after night as
we lock ourselves down.
Just him & me and me & him.
He is in my space and I in his.
We find quiet places
alone, together, to disappear.
Some days neither has room
for another human soul.
He wears me down with his words.
They are too loud, indiscriminate.
He doesn't ask permission
to interrupt my inner world.
Other days, he is a shelter.
He holds me when the tears flow
for my boy, our son, so far, far away.
Often, he is stupid and absurd
and sometimes I adore his absurdity
and other times I sigh deeply
and repeat the words,
'be patient, be kind,' and
then I realise that he too
knows this mantra well.
Together we cook and clean
and sleep and dream.
Together we lose our days and
at night we lose our sleep.
His snore proclaims
'I am here, I am alive,' but still

I rehearse his Coronavirus death.
The version where he is alone
and so am I.
And then we weep some more for all
the pain and loss in the world.
But we live another isolation day.
A day of nothing very meaningful at all.
And sometimes we remember gratitude.
We remind ourselves that trivial incidentals
are important in the span of a human life.
And thus he is with me always, but not forever.
His body, his breath, his 'himness'.
We are not apart and I am blessed.

Alison Bromley
I am a retired teaching assistant and have been married 40 years; I enjoy art, writing and journalling. Walking and getting outdoors has been my salvation during lockdown!

The Garden

I can feel the heat of the day as I water our newly planted garden. Roses scent the warmth of the spring evening air as the spray from the hose turns into rainbows. I turn to quench the thirsty vegetable beds, beans waving brightly bi-coloured flowers in the gentle breeze, no signs yet of the delicious treats to come. The squash and courgette are growing well, with flower buds starting to appear. I have a strong feeling the blackbird may have been the strawberry thief who has taken the almost ripe berries. I must remember to find some cover tomorrow. The bees buzzing drowsily in the bells of foxgloves brings me back to now, the joy of the moment gone in a blink.

My thoughts run away again, my daughter in hospital with her newborn child. No visitors for her, after two weeks of what must feel like a lifetime in a very lonely place. No coos, no ahhs for the pretty child sleeping peacefully in her hospital crib. No proud dad and husband bringing flowers and balloons to cheer my daughter in those hormonal weepy moments that follow birth, as surely as night follows day. Her heartsore longing for home and some sort of normality... she must be concerned for her two-year-old at home, wondering where her mummy has gone.

We can do nothing.
Just stay home. Stay safe.

I find myself standing with the water running into a pool at my feet. Shaking myself from these thoughts I carry on with the task in hand, my feet now wet and sticky. Clematis are climbing the metal arch, not bad progress for less than a year. I feel calm and serene again. Gardens do that. Green space brings serenity and peace. Tomato, cucumber, melons are next on the list for hydration after the heat of the day... they visibly perk up with the cooling shower of water. Task completed.

Slowly wandering back to the house, I check all the plants are well and happy, deadheading spent blooms as I go. A bat flits past as the light is fading now. The whites and blues of blooms come alive, almost glow as the light fades... the last triumph of the spring day.

Just more of the same tomorrow, I think. More of the same.

A phone trills – my phone. My son – job lost, like our freedom, lost in the blink of an eye. He tried so hard to find this job. He is putting on a brave face to this loss, but he has a family to feed, a mortgage to pay, a wife working on the front line of this virus war we are all fighting. 'We'll manage,' he says. 'We'll be fine.'

I know him. These are his brave words. His 'Don't you worry, Mum,' words. The very words which will keep him awake at night with anxiety.

I must stay at home, stay safe, protect our NHS.

I cannot even give him a hug. Cannot go and visit, talk things out. Cannot look into his eyes to know what he is going through. I look through the window and the garden beckons. I wander out with my thoughts. The garden wraps me in its healing embrace, a warm blanket trying to replace the real contact of kith and kin, a poor substitute. Darkness has descended but the warm scents of a beautiful day surround me, slowly bringing calm and order to my thoughts and feelings.

Gardens are healing, rejuvenating spaces. I cannot imagine my life without my 'me' space, my 'peace' place, my 'restoring my soul' place. We are so lucky to have our own very beautiful space. We may have to stay home to stay safe and protect our NHS, but we have our very own green oasis to help us through this horrible time. Many do not, and I wonder how they are managing. How do you keep little ones safe at home with no outdoor play and place to explore? Is screen time their happy place? I hope not. All our lives are on hold, as if a pause button has been pressed. The youngest amongst us cannot understand what is happening, why today is so different to yesterday.

Tomorrow we will be back in our paradise garden, toiling, sowing, planting, watering... because we must stay home.

The world will go on turning. The virus will carry on spreading. Our leaders will continue to make mistakes that are costing thousands of innocent lives, putting wealth before health and forgetting to care. Our essential workers will carry on carrying on, worrying about the risk they face everyday to themselves and their family. Will we remember them at the end of this, as surely this must come to an end.

We, we will stay at home because we must.
We, we will stay strong because we must.

Jill Brown

Born, educated, worked and live in Coventry... I am retired, married with a large family of five children and eleven grandchildren, who live far and wide. I am immensely proud of all of them. I love cooking, and baking, watercolor painting, sewing, reading and of course gardening.

Favourite Day

My favourite day was Thursday,
I'd set out just past nine,
to catch the bus to art class
and be there in good time.
We'd sit around and chatter
about last week's piece of art,
lovely to see other people's work,
I think they're very smart.
A lesson next on this week's task,
a demo and advice,
and off we go to start our piece,
I hope it turns out nice!
We paint and chat with all our friends,
our time there just flies by,
then it's 'See you next week and thanks,'
as we all say 'Goodbye '.
But now it's gone,
the art class is no more.
Coronavirus stalks the Earth
and keeps us all indoors.
Painting alone is not the same,
no camaraderie or tea,
I hope when normal times return
there's an art class there for me.

Joyce Porritt

I was born in Coventry in 1944, left to study at London University and after raising a family in Kent returned to the city in 2000. I'm passionate about all things science... and of course, I love my art class.

Lockdown Acrostic

Love dwelling in our hearts and in our homes
Opportunity to learn a new skill
Celebrate when it's all over
Keep up the positivity, this won't last forever
Don't stop working hard, we'll soon be back at school
Out and about for an hour a day
We are all in this together
NHS – thank you!

Fearne Parham, age 10

I love acting and singing, but I have really missed family and friends (and even school) throughout lockdown. I can't wait to see everyone again.

It Just Takes a Smile...

12th March 2020, 10:37pm

'Whoooooosshhhh!' The sound of rain battling with the earth disturbed the silence. No one spoke. 'Beep... beep... beep... beep... beep... beep...'

Silence.

The day was gloomy, dark, sorrowful. That was the day my mum died. She was a nurse working at St Thomas's Hospital in London... she would always come back home smiling and showing off about how her day was amazing, meeting new people and having a laugh about a not-so-funny joke that she and her colleagues had come up with.

Yes, occasionally she would be in tears because someone had just died, or because a favourite patient had left the hospital. For me, those moments were the best because me and my little sister would hug her tight and cry together, knowing how incredibly brave our mum was. Time would stop and we would feel connected again, in a deeper world where it was just us.

After our period of breaking down, we would sit together, the three of us, and laugh at old childhood memories whilst our mum caressed us. Then our dad would barge in, home from his shift, and plunge in too, rolling around making loud noises. We would scold him for interrupting but laugh with leaping hearts as we cuddled together.

Later, we would disperse into our own little worlds: I would run to the bedroom to finish off my homework, my sister would be in hers, grooming all her freaky French dolls. My dad would be downstairs, shouting cringey dad-puns, and Mum would be in the kitchen trying not to laugh while making dinner.

Typical.

Every day was the same. I never thought that things could change so drastically. It never crossed my mind. Negativity was never an option in our family – 'Think positive and smile,' was our motto. So, when misery crept its way into my mind, I would think positive: family, love, true happiness – all things required in human life. It helped a lot, especially for a 15-year-old girl battling with her own problems.

But I guess it made me overlook a part of life that is incredibly important: that period where everything falls apart. Where you crouch down slowly at the painful feeling of your heart being chained, your neck strangled, your head heavy.

I don't know whether I felt this way before, but after my mum's death, it hit me brutally and I realised all of the pain my mum felt as a nurse. She hid it well.

24th February 2020

'Good morning, it is currently 7:30am. The total deaths in the UK has risen to 990 with 40 deaths reported yesterday due to the Covid-19 disease...'

'More deaths!' whined my sister as she stuck herself to Mum.

'Mum, I do hope you are being careful... just don't go, please?' I pleaded.

'Oh, stop it both of you! You know I must go – they need me more than ever! This is all I can do. Now get off, I need to go in a second.'

'Just promise me that you won't go into the intensive care section...'

'I promise.'

It's better to hear how a lie is easily made than to know the true meaning behind it. It's like a part in a sad movie that everyone misses but then realises at the end when it's too late. They take it for granted, not thinking about the worst – but when it happens, suddenly it's unbearable to watch. 'If only she did not go... oh, I get it now... awwwww...' They are phrases only said at the end, when the movie finishes, later forgotten about and left to die.

I wish it was a movie. I wish that everything could fall back to normal when the cameras turn off.

Mum lied. Turns out that this time, she wasn't OK. The shadow had taken over and she surrendered, the shadow that ran with the wind, taking down every innocent leaf from its tree.

Covid-19. A disease, a demon running on the surface of the earth. It either took down lives or changed them drastically – everyone had to stay at home, no GCSE for year 11 or A-Level for year 12, no school, no social interaction, more deaths, including the death of my mum.

That was the last time I saw my mum well.

I blame myself for not noticing the symptoms, the sudden chill I always had, the painful lines embedded on her soft face. I blame myself.

She stopped coming home, said the risk was too great. Quick phone calls and empty 'I love yous' was all we got from her, until the 11th of March when we were told that she had the disease and was not going to make it.

Until that moment, it was a blur. Like I purposely fast forwarded it to avoid sudden heart drops, but this one scene I remember so clearly: I was slowly walking into the intensive care room, wearing full protection, taking one step at a time until I reached the bed where she lay.

'M-mum?' I stuttered, as tears blurred my vision.

'Oh, my beauty... don't come too close now,' she said softly.

'Mum... you promised me! Why? Why did you break your promise? You're leaving us... how are we going to manage without you, Mum? H-how?'

She smiled.

'Go... look in the mirror. It just takes a smile, Sarah. A smile....'

12th March 2020, 10:37pm

Anne Adegbenle

I am a student at Bishop Ullathorne School and once met Cathy Cassidy when she visited my primary school. I've never stopped writing since then!

Lockdown Life

Everyday feels the same,
the same boring day
trapped inside your house…
the constant temptation to walk away.

It feels like it's been forever,
yes, I am aware.
The whole world's on pause for a deadly virus,
and that is something rare.

I look at the world,
and there is less to be seen.
There is not much to do now,
just stare at your screen.

The shops are empty
along with the streets…
we stay home, trying to entertain ourselves
but the same boring day just repeats.

Don't take the risk…
staying at home is for the best.
Covid-19 is beyond our control.
Can we overcome it? It's all a test.

Grace Sharman, age 13

I live with my mum, dad, two brothers and a sister and although I work hard in all my subjects, my main interest is sports, netball especially. I'd love to follow this up as a career one day, perhaps as a teacher.

Living in the Countryside

The countryside is everywhere
where humankind is not
though lonely houses sparsely stand
the land is nature's cot.
Nowhere is without some life,
be it foxes, bugs or plants –
through rolling hills and luscious woods
and soggy, damp wetlands.
Some may find a safe haven
within these grassy plains,
why not take a shot at life
for death the body pains?
Here in morbid quarantine
our houses are our graves,
so let us run to rolling hills
away from modern caves.

Rudy Wheatley de Groot, age 12

I live in Coventry with my brother Arthur and twin sister Dora, and have been enjoying not going to school during lockdown. I like drawing cartoons, walking in the woods and talking to my friends on Whatsapp.

Mimi

It was early one morning when I heard something coming from my wardrobe. Since this was around the time when we were stuck at home due to the lockdown, I hoped that it was something exciting. As I drew closer, I noticed that some of my clothes at the bottom of the closet were shuffling around. My hand reached over and grabbed one of my shoes to use as self-defence. Slowly lifting the clothes with my hand, the shoe clutched tightly in the other, I peered closer, and out jumped a tiny kitten, dangerously thin.

I picked the kitten up carefully and stroked her soft fur as she purred in gratitude. Placing her in the wardrobe once again, I heard her stomach make a low grumbling noise.

'You're hungry, aren't you? Don't worry, I'll bring you some food to eat!'

I checked the Internet to see what kittens like to eat, and I brought her some milk with water in it. After that, I went over to my computer to complete my homework for the day, wondering what I could do to hide her from my parents. I was sure that they wouldn't be so eager to keep a cat in the house – it would be one extra mouth to feed. When I was done thinking about it, I decided that I would call her Mimi.

Over time, Mimi and I grew closer than ever and eventually I picked up the courage to tell my parents about her. Thankfully, they were understanding and allowed me to keep her, because after all I had been taking care of her for so long already.

Every now and then I would take food up to her and stroke her as she slept. One day as I went to my bedroom with a tin of sardines for her to eat, I looked for Mimi... but she was gone!

Looking around to see if there was any trace of her, I found muddy paw prints leading outside and over the fence. She was gone, and there was nothing that I could do about it. Mimi had gone, but with her help I had made the most of my time during lockdown.

I love you Mimi... and that wardrobe door is always open, just in case!

Maame McSam, age 12

Four-Year-Old Fun in the Lockdown Sun

Mum and dad have told me that the germs have shut my school,
now I get to spend all day with them, and that is really cool.
When I get up in the morning, I find dad works from our house –
so when he's on the telephone, I'm as quiet as a mouse.

I love that he is always here, at breakfast, lunch and dinner –
this new world the germ made is certainly a winner!
My mum's not working anymore – and this is really great!
Even my baby sister wants to be my new best mate.

We do lots of cool stuff every day like drawing, sticking, baking.
We've even done some messy gloop and sock-bunny making!
I do dance on Zoom and even had a virtual party invitation –
and the whole street got together for a special celebration.

I go for walks in the country, sometimes twice a day,
I stroke all the horses (they like to say 'neigh.')
I'm growing out of all my clothes, and into other sizes,
I've also learnt to ride my bike without its stabilisers!

I miss my other family and all my friends at school,
I miss going to the park and swimming at the pool...
I miss going on holidays and having lots of fun,
but at least the germs came when we had a lot of sun!

Sam Merrick

I live in Allesley, Coventry, with my fiancée Alicia and daughters Iris and Penny. I work locally at Coventry Building Society and enjoy football and watching the NFL in my spare time. I write the odd poem for family and friends... this one is for my eldest daughter, Iris, who inspired the poem.

Becoming… and Simply Being

I became a student and I knew it all,
then Covid-19 struck
and I knew nothing at all.
My steady emotions began to unravel
to an unexpected resolve.

How one can be so busy
that time is meaningful
to meaningless unresolve.

Who am I?
Started work, lost
and begun another job
all in a daily jog.

The space of three months
has taught me to remember, remember
the 15th of November
(my birthday).

No – remember, remember to wash your hands,
wear your mask
and keep your distance.

I wonder will you simply be,
not like you but like me?

For hope and prosperity let's see…
will you become and simply be?

Zia Arif
I have a diploma in Career Guidance and am currently working as a Case Manager. I live with my twin sister, love knitting and dressmaking and am also trained in professional hair and make-up.

a song of hope

folks talk and post 'bout the virus, matters serious and grave
but you want pictures of happy times, times of untainted joy
so I'm sat on the floor with old albums unwrapping memories we made
I was young, I had a 'tache, and you were my little boy.

ain't it funny how an old photo can turn your world upside down?
a tremor, shake and a fearful ache to take you all in my arms
so I go slightly to pieces and crumple to the floor
while the blackbird sings atop the chimney pot,
a song of hope falls soft into our home.

we talk quite often on face-time, zoom in and out of each others' lives
it don't add up to what we miss the most, hug's tender clutch.
I knew this was true, thought it obvious, though its force I never realised
'til I sat on that floor and let the tears fall
in the place left where there should have been touch.

we meet sometimes over the gate, at a distance deemed to be safe
a strange sort of refuge, sat on the drive, but a comfort and no harm.
she was walking, sobbing and shaking, found herself in that place
got out her phone and you went to near her
and brought her to some sort of calm.

ain't it funny how an old photo can turn your world upside down?
a tremor, shake and a fearful ache to take you all in my arms
so I go slightly to pieces and crumple to the floor
while the blackbird sings atop the chimney pot,
a song of hope to carry us on.

Michael Luntley

we should have built you palaces...

boxes in the air, boxes in the air
the planners didn't think it through, them in charge forget to care
in times of plague and lockdown and trying to keep safe
you're fifteen floors to heaven, there's no haven in this place.

the roof it is off limits, the lift don't go up and down
it's thirty flights of stairwell to get you to the ground
you carry toddler and buggy down three hundred stairs
tho' there ain't no play equipment or seating for you there.

boxes in the air, boxes in the air
the planners didn't think it through, them in charge forget to care
in times of plague and lockdown and trying to keep safe
you're fifteen floors to heaven, there's no haven in this place.

could have had a gym, a pool and bar up on the roof
a high wall of safety glass and a panoramic view
they might do that for fancy folk, brushed chrome and large glass plate
even though when all is said and done, it's just another pile of crates.

boxes in the air, boxes in the air
the planners didn't think it through, them in charge forget to care
in times of plague and lockdown and trying to keep safe
you're fifteen floors to heaven, there's no haven in this place.

you need privacy and quiet to make a box a home
but you get fights, screams and arguments and occasional lovers' moans.
kids next door have gone feral jumping off table, beds and chairs
they're all bouncing off the walls of your boxes in the air.

boxes in the air, boxes in the air
the planners didn't think it through, them in charge forget to care
in times of plague and lockdown and trying to keep safe
you're fifteen floors to heaven, there's no haven in this place.

Grenfell's lessons ain't been learned, ain't been taken to heart
pile 'em high and neglect them seems the politician's art
I wish that I could take you away to gardens fair
respite for you and yours from your boxes in the air.

boxes in the air, boxes in the air
the planners didn't think it through, them in charge forget to care
in times of plague and lockdown and trying to keep safe
you're fifteen floors to heaven, there's no haven in this place.

some think there's nothing to be done, it's just how these things are
but how things are is how we make them, it's up to us to set the bar
and if you wouldn't want this for your friends or for your kin
how come that it's acceptable for those who live within?

boxes in the air, boxes in the air
the planners didn't think it through, them in charge forgot to care
if we had had compassion for those who lived and still live there
we could have built you palaces, we should have built you palaces,
we should have built you palaces not boxes in the air.

yeah, we should have built you palaces.

Michael Luntley

I took early retirement from academia and fill time as music promoter (Sheep Dip Sessions) and singer/songwriter and occasional poet; wrote and produced show 'from this ground', a set of six songs and five poems (Olga Dermott-Bond) on themes of identity, belonging and migration based on research on emigration of agricultural labourers and their families to Brazil in 1872/73. The show premiered late 2019 and is booked to appear at studio space, Coventry Albany Theatre in April 2021.

Unspoken Words

I remember the first time I laid eyes on you. It was a beautiful day in November; clear skies and a crisp, cold wind that threatened snow. I looked up and there you were, across the park on roller skates. You, too, looked up – our eyes locked. It could have been a second or a hundred seconds; all I knew was I never wanted to look away. Then your friend nudged your shoulder and we tore our eyes apart.

I came back to that park as often as possible, sitting on that same bench. Ridiculous, isn't it? I don't know what I expected. There was something about you... your piercing eyes, the intensity of our gaze... I was drawn to you. Clichéd, I know.

Over the next few weeks, I found myself looking for you everywhere. I sought your gaze in the crowds I walked through. I searched for your face at the protests I went to, but to no avail.

The next time I saw you, I was sitting in a coffee shop. You were outside, with the same friend from the park, about to cross the road. Our eyes locked again – I felt the same breathlessness I did before, and I watched as your friend pulled you across the road, throwing you an irritated look.

The first time we met is ingrained in my memory. I was walking down the street when we collided. You were on roller skates again, your arms flailing as I knocked you off balance. Without hesitation, I grabbed you to steady you, and we stood there for a moment. We'd locked eyes so many times before, a connection formed by mystery and some unknown attraction.

There were a thousand unspoken words between us.

'Hi,' I breathed.
'It's you,' you marvelled.

We exchanged numbers and went our separate ways. We spent weeks texting before we saw each other. The next few weeks were a blur of winter magic and long conversations. Before I knew what was happening, I found myself falling for you.

I remember when you asked if you could kiss me. I leaned forward, gently pressing my mouth to yours as I cupped your face. Your breath hitched the moment our lips touched, before you gripped my shoulder and kissed me back. When I pulled away to rest my forehead against yours, you wrapped your arms around my neck and kissed me again.

I remember when you asked me if I'd like to go on a date with you, a flush creeping up your neck. You couldn't look me in the eye, examining your shoes. You met my gaze with surprise when I answered yes, eyes lighting up.

I remember when you asked me to be yours, exclusively. Winter had been chased by spring, that magnificent time of year when summer was just around the corner, the promise of warmer days and freedom.

And then the pandemic hit. We were separated to different sides of the city, our plans broken. Not only was the city on lock-down, but so were our hearts. FaceTime and midnight texts had nothing on human touch. I felt sick inside, and it had nothing to do with the virus.

I remember when I awoke to your text proposing we meet, social distancing-style. I was ecstatic, buzzing for days. I couldn't touch you, not even a kiss, but I could see you smile and hear that laugh in real life.

I remember walking past armed policemen, wondering why they needed guns to ensure social distancing. It was more than likely just to threaten the public. My heart skipped a beat when you waved to me from the other side of the park. Walking past the other people milling about, I didn't know you had but mere minutes left.

I remember the last day of your life, although it's a blank in my mind; a series of flashes of moments. The police officers. The guns. The bullets that entered your body, one after the other. Blood. Screaming. Your body going limp. The cop that held me back when I tried to get to you. The cop handcuffing me after I tried to lunge at the cop that shot you.

I remember the days after. Everything felt surreal. I spent most of my time lumbering around, staring blankly. None of it felt real.

I remember when it hit me. Suddenly I was back to that day, reaching for you as they dragged me away, your body limp and bloody on the ground. You were gone. Dead. I lay in bed all day and sobbed until my throat was raw. I didn't know how to breathe without you, how to fill the you-sized hole left in my heart. I would never again see you smile. I would never again hear you laugh.

The real virus tearing through the world isn't Covid-19 but racism, the hate so much of this world is built on. You were violently ripped from the world. Your heart was torn from mine. You were taken from the world with a thousand things you hadn't done, a thousand unspoken words still on your tongue.

My heart still hurts, but the pain and anguish that choked me has slowly ebbed to a dull ache, making room for the fire that burns uncontrollably deep within. I am angry. I am angry because your murderers went home to their families and won't pay for their actions. I am angry because your murderers are responsible for upholding justice – but only when it fits their viewpoint. I am angry because you were murdered for nothing other than being a black man in America. I am angry because they would have shot me too, if my skin wasn't white. I am angry because yours isn't the only life lost like this. I am angry because our eyes will never again meet across the park.

I remember the first time I laid eyes on you…

K. Sehmi, age 15

I'm a proud feminist, with ambitions of becoming an author. I hate seagulls and I love cows. I have a little sister, and my family has basically adopted my best friend as my second sister.

Staying Inside

Sitting, rocking, standing,
walking, jumping, playing,
climbing, baking, sleeping,
waking, working, listening,
writing, looking, talking,
waving, stopping, loving,
clapping, wishing, missing,
hoping, waiting, calling.

Monday: waking up dreading the hours of work ahead.
Waiting for someone to answer a call.
Working for hours non-stop.
Wishing to see my loved ones again.

Tuesday: listening to the voices I love the most.
Jumping up and down, up and down on the trampoline.
Sleeping more and less everyday.
Writing a postcard to cheer someone up.

Wednesday: standing still not knowing where to go.
Rocking on the swing is so relaxing.
Walking around the park smiling at the faces I don't even know.

Thursday: stopping and just thinking.
Talking to neighbours that have become family.
Clapping for the nurses and doctors saving all of us.
Missing those we've all lost.

Friday: climbing into the tent to have a garden camping trip.
Sitting watching a film snuggled up with my family.
Hoping that everyone is staying safe.
Loving more than ever before.

Saturday: baking more and more every day.
Waving through the window to everyone.
Playing with board games around the table

Sunday: calling everyone to carry on with church.
Laughing with everyone on all the zoom quizzes.
Looking through memories from many years ago.

Staying inside isn't that bad...
as long as I'm in contact with all the people I love.

Poppy Burgess, age 13

I enjoy baking, reading, photography and spending time with family and friends. This poem won my school's Year Eight lockdown competition, and I was able to perform it on the BBC CWR Lockdown Upload programme!

Prison

Lockdown is like prison,
outside so far yet near,
but all souls are lucky that today they have risen –
the mourning of lost loved ones is all that we hear.

Lockdown is like prison,
a cage for all of us.
The government make the weekly rules,
no trains, no planes, no bus.

Lockdown is like prison,
but there is a key –
the NHS has given this –
stay at home, their plea.

Winnie Wainaina, age 12
I am a student at Bishop Ullathorne School and my favourite subject is English – I love to read and write. I have one older sister who is 15.

Mysterious Invasion

Our life was happy and carefree... we had wonderful friends, nice teachers at school and a lot of fun each day. Then everything changed. There appeared a monstrous monster from nowhere - his name was Covid. The beast was enormous. He looked horrible, with red, fierce eyes and fangs that were dirty and sharp as shark's teeth. His intention was to gain power over the planet Earth.

First he attacked China and then moved to invade other countries. He wanted more, more, more. All over the world, people were scared of the monster and locked themselves in their own houses. They were afraid to leave home, as the monster had the ability to move with the speed of light and could appear in any place, at anytime.

Some people who faced the monster managed to escape, but suffered many wounds as a result. Some were murdered, and some were lucky not to meet the villain at all. In a short period of time our lives shrank. We had only our house and garden, which became our fortress. We decided to protect our fortress, and if we have to face the monstrous monster we will fight him like real soldiers.

We know that one day, from the rainbow, there will appear a white knight riding a white unicorn who will defeat the villain and save humanity. Our life will be back to normal.

Wictor Novak, age 8 & Oliwia Novak, age 7

We go to St Augustine's Primary. Polish is our first language, but we both love to read and invent stories in English too! Wictor loves maths and Oliwia prefers arts, crafts and dancing, but we both love books. Our mum Magdalena helped us to put together this story.

Changes

From quickly getting up in the morning and rushing to uni lectures, to just rolling over on my bed, switching my laptop on and clicking Zoom.

From attending my weekly women's group every Thursday, to weekly Zoom calls and just chatting away about everything freely.

From going out to Ramadan gatherings at feast time, to delivering the food to people's doorsteps.

From going out and doing fun stuff on my birthday, to staying in and receiving gifts through the post, delivering my birthday cake to my loved ones and just enjoying my quarantine birthday.

From thinking 2020 would be a calm year, to knowing it's been far from that.

From an innocent person being killed, to a major mass movement started across the world.

From having less knowledge on certain things that can make various people uncomfortable, to actually learning about it and understanding what certain demographic groups go through.

From just looking after my own family and making sure everything is on the table, to actually looking out for neighbours who are living on their own and making them feel part of the family and making sure they are OK.

From thinking life is going too fast and there's no time to catch up, to life just slowing down and just appreciating every moment.

Just learn to appreciate life and live the moments with family and friends, even if it is in a socially distanced type of way, because no one knows when the almighty will pick your soul up and take you away with him.

Amaara Arif
I have just recently finished university and like writing poetry in my spare time – it's a form of expression for me, I release everything onto paper. I like painting also because it's like taking the image out of my brain and putting it into the colours. Baking is one of my favourite hobbies – who doesn't love cake!

Lockdown Blues

This lockdown's a bit of a do –
and of course, the pandemic too.
But I do declare
it's the state of my hair
about which I haven't a clue!

One morning how blue was the air...
my frustration I really must share!
'Twas not very kindly
of my phone to remind me
of an appointment that's no longer there!

My husband is in deep depression –
you can tell by his real glum expression!
One day the hairdressers
may tackle his tresses –
but right now he wants hair in recession!

I spotted a cure for his ills
which didn't involve taking pills!
Only wanted to help
but he let out a yelp
and promptly ran for the hills!

The cutter they market's a charm,
I'd be happy to chance my arm –
bald bits and tufts?
A refugee from Crufts?
I don't think I'd do any harm!

He offered to practise on me –
but that's quite different you see!
Although it's ten weeks
without trims, without tweaks
I think I will just let things be!

Oh dear, how my barnet has grown –
like a lawn that has yet to be mown!
It could save me a task
and be used as a mask –
now I look like a Chewbacca clone!

So, my hair now feels like a hat
and I'm getting increasingly fat.
With more crisps and more gin
I will never be thin –
my waistline don't know where it's at.

Six packs of Maltesers a pound –
look what a bargain I've found!
I'll hide them away
and scoff one a day
so it won't my diet confound!

Now I come to my final complaint –
third and last in the picture I paint!
Who made the decree
there'd be no place to pee?
It would try the patience of a saint!

Spend a penny in the open air?
It's not an experience to share!
I'd feel quite harassed
and then embarrassed
getting caught with pants down and bum bare!

I suppose I could find a big tree,
but what of my arthritic knee?
Grab, point and shoot
really don't suit
the female anatomy!

These are the most difficult of days,
for our forbearance we deserve praise.
But peeing al fresco
on the way back from Tesco
will not be my latest craze!

For now, I'll say a fond farewell
as we navigate out of this hell –
if we just survive
and thank God we're alive
that outcome would suit me just swell!

Beth Hill

I am a retired foreign languages teacher and have always enjoyed writing stories and poems. During lockdown, I've had a limerick challenge going with a friend who is shielding – we've exchanged limericks every day and I am now up to 1,778! It keeps me out of mischief!

The Protectors

The creature dashed into the undergrowth of the miniature jungle. The creature thought it was hidden, but I could see it clearly. I got low to the ground like a snake, waiting for my chance to pounce, licking my lips in anticipation. Very quietly and slowly I inched forward, staying as low as I could, hoping for some camouflage from the towering foliage. The creature squeaked and twitched, feeling my presence but unable to see me. My chance was here and I had to take it. I pushed back on my hind legs and leapt forward – only to be stopped in my tracks by a jingling noise.

I knew that noise, and in excitement I dashed back home and soared through my little door. In the middle of the hallway they stood, my protectors. They had returned from their daily voyage.

I greeted them my usual way and stretched myself out on the sun warmed carpet for some well-deserved belly rubs. This had been our daily routine ever since my protectors had brought me into their compound. The love which radiated from them was a drastic contrast to the brutality I had experienced before coming into their care. My previous protector hadn't been as nice to me.

From the prison of his care, I then ended up in an actual prison called The Cattery. I had been arrested for some crime I didn't commit – but at least I had been removed from the clutches of evil. I wasn't in The Cattery for long, and to be honest, it wasn't all that bad. The guards were upbeat and the food was delicious.

I met a lot of others like me in The Cattery, all having been through some sort of hardship. We passed our time talking through the fences that divided us and got to know each other – where we had come from, where we wanted to go. There was one fellow prisoner that I was truly sad to leave behind – the black and white one called Tibbles. He was a warrior, and he bore the scars to prove it. Despite his burly exterior and his one eye, he was as soft as fresh tuna from the tin. Tibbles spent many evenings coaching me on my hunting technique, practicing on the little fuzzy pink ball the guards had kindly provided.

Our time was cut short – it seemed I was one of the chosen ones. My new protectors had come to free me from the manacles of injustice and bring me to their empire of love. I had left Tibbles behind but I swore I'd find him again one day. Maybe my protectors would care for him too?

Since then, my protectors have gone on daily voyages called 'work' and often bring back goods from foreign lands. The best I can do to thank them for all their generosity is to use the skills Tibbles taught me and capture the pesky creatures that plague our jungle of pines, bringing back their bodies like trophies to please them. When I succeed, I am often greeted by screams of joy as they jump onto nearby furnishings in happiness. Our companionship is equal, we provide for each other.

'That's it, Marcie! Schools are closed, I can't go to work!' exclaimed my female protector, caressing my face...

'Corona has locked down the world,' replied my male protector. Corona has locked down the world? Both of them went on in deep discussion about this Corona, coming to sit in front of the vision box to listen to their blond-haired leader explain the threat we were now under. The leader said Corona was serious and we were being asked to stay inside and never leave. Corona was killing people...

My mind began to race. We needed to act now, not stay inside! I attempted to communicate with my protectors, jumping up into their laps, but it was like they were in a trance. This was serious. Why weren't they moving into action? Was their job not to protect? We couldn't just sit at home like we were being ordered to do!

'Well, that's that then,' my male protector stated. 'We're going nowhere! Might as well binge watch Tiger King...'

I was horrified to see my protectors become so relaxed in a moment like this. This was a national emergency and they wanted to watch a show about some man with a mullet and my far distant cousins? Corona had obviously corrupted my protectors – and their leaders.

This was serious. I didn't know who this Corona was, but I knew in that moment, as I watched my protectors sink deeper into their seats, that it was my time to become the protector.

And I needed Tibbles...

Ashleigh Francis

I'm 24 years old, living with my boyfriend and our cat, Marceline. I have always loved reading and writing... anything creative I can get my hands on really! I studied theatre and performed most of my life but am now training to be an English teacher. I love cats, musicals, video games, books, music, binge watching shows on Netflix and a bunch of other weird and nerdy stuff.

Alone

The days are long, I feel alone,
my contacts now are just by phone.
The streets are quiet – few cars run
but I can hear the blackbird's song,
they sing out loud those little birds
as all is quiet they can be heard.
I try to be grateful for the little things,
the joy I feel when the telephone rings.
I speak to family and to friends
and for a few moments the loneliness ends.
We laugh together at little things
no-one knows what joy that brings.
When all this ends – no doubt it will –
normal things will please me still,
shopping trips and lunches out
will all resume without a doubt.
These lonesome days will then be gone
normal life again... bring it on!

Pat Rogers

I'm 72 years of age and live alone with my dog. I have two daughters who are both frontline nurses.

...castling...

A garden full of roses,
a junket full of posers...
he misused the issues,
but hasn't fallen down;
but should.
They've broken the trust of a nation,
by going station to station,
but a castle didn't fall down!
I'm only going to test my eyes!
It's sparked a conversation with the lies,
they're going wherever they want to go...
they may fall down!
The lockdown's become quantitative easing,
people still control their sneezing,
as schools wait to reopen,
where will they sit down?
Social distancing will be hard to keep,
as truth, in government, is only skin-deep,
a tissue of lies and mistruths,
will they all fall down?
It's too early to raise the limbo bar,
cabinet ministers showing who they are:
a ballyhoo, no value,
perhaps they'll all fall down!

Peter Longden

I am married with two grown up sons, Ben, a graphic designer for the Guardian; and Joe, a mature student of English and Creative Writing. I had a long, varied career in the Youth Service, retiring in 2017 to focus on my writing. I love cooking, live music, theatre and sport, especially rugby. My own sports were basketball and volleyball, and these days I try to keep fit by walking and cycling. I'm also learning to speak Argentine Spanish.

Bee Thing

Last summer a bee got tangled in my hair
and we both panicked and it stung me.
I know bees are good; no bees, no food.
No bees, no flowers or trees –
but I don't want bees anywhere near me.

We were outside in the back yard, locked down, quarantined.
My mum was sick with the virus, in a plastic chair, just sitting
and all I could hear was bees buzzing everywhere.
I couldn't deal with it, I had to go in.

And my parents got cross
You've never been afraid of bees before! they said,
as if that meant I was never allowed to be afraid of bees.
I keep hearing buzzing and it's making me jumpy!
Bees do not respect two metre personal boundaries!

Later, they thought about it and decided
that maybe the bee thing is more about
the fact that Mum is ill and soon I might be.
(Everything is about the virus these days.)

Maybe there are too many questions and worries
and every new news story about deaths and vulnerabilities
brings new, invisible might-bees
that have me flailing around uncertainly.

In the meantime, though,
I can't be doing with bees.

Andrea Mbarushimana
I am a poet, artist and Grapevine community connector, working from home with my husband and daughter. I wrote this poem for children and young people struggling with quarantine. www.andrea-mbarushimana.com

First Day Back

First day back to school today,
my tummy feels all funny.
Can't wait to see all my friends again
but something is wrong with Mummy.

First day back to school today,
no photo by the front door.
Mummy said, 'No, not today...'
but why I'm not quite sure.

First day back to school today,
can't wait to play with you...
I'll squish you with my best hug
And share my toys, it's true!

First day back at school today,
we lined up by the gate.
I spotted Fred, I tried to run
but Mummy shouted 'Wait!'

First day back to school today,
I waved goodbye to Mummy.
A little tear rolled down her cheek...
the ache grew in my tummy.

First day back to school today,
I'm no longer in Fred's class.
Miss explained, 'We cannot mix!'
as I peered through the glass.

First day back to school today,
I tripped and grazed my knee –
Miss stayed back as she wiped it clean.
Why is she scared of me?

First day back to school today,
I learnt how not to share –
and how to stay away from friends,
to show them that I care.

First day back to school today,
my teacher waved goodbye
Mummy wrapped me in her arms
as we both tried not to cry.

Chloe Griffiths, age 14, Stoke Park School

Message

Hi guys,
I have some bad news.
I understand you'd made lots of plans, but c'mon –
we are already five months in –
face the facts. It's kinda gone a bit downhill.
This Corona stuff was only supposed to last a week.
This was supposed to teach you all a lesson –
stop destroying my life's works.
I might as well have just sent down
some asteroids or something instead.
You are doing this all WRONG –
stay inside,
wash your hands!
After a lot of consideration, I've decided to postpone 2020.
We will continue next year...
peace out.
God x

Trinity Douglas, age 15, Stoke Park School

Remember

Remember last year
saying 2020 is going to be the year...
the year of what?
Year of nothing, nobody and nonsense.
Think about when Sophie called
just to show you she was making pancakes,
think about your 'best friends'
that you haven't heard a word from in two months,
think about the deep late-night conversations
you had with your best friend
about what you are actually gonna do with your life.
Please look back on these times
and remember this one time
you could actually help save the world.

Trinity Douglas, age 15, Stoke Park School

Lockdown Blues

Lockdown has started,
it feels like we parted.
Lockdown has started,
time has darted.

The days slide away,
with lightning speed.
It can be boring, it can be fun,
we follow lockdown's lead.

Has a month ever felt this long?
It feels like we are trapped in a song.
We do not ask to be a part of history,
yet here we are.

Lockdown has started,
days are passing.
Lockdown has started,
it feels like we parted.

Kareena Patria, age 13, Stoke Park School

'Beat the Devil Out of It'

Lockdown sanity saved by a man from the past.
His soothing voice, talk of happy places to put a tree,
wielding a two-inch paintbrush and palette knife
with the abandoned grace only a craftsman can achieve.
During those 7pm slices of time
I forgot staying 2m apart, endless hand washing,
wiping the baked bean tin just in case,
after a hasty shop masked and gloved.
For those 30 minutes, mountains emerged, water rippled,
lay of the land explained, forests rapidly grew.
I wondered if odourless thinner was odourless,
made a mental note, Thalo Green is a powerful colour,
and how to flatten paint and get that little roll of paint on your knife.
He created happy clouds, sunsets and snow scenes
with a reassuring familiarity.
Washing brushes was a highlight ending the process,
where he'd 'beat the Devil out of it' on his easel.
More than his painting it was his reassurance in a world
constantly looking over its shoulder.
This kindly, softly spoken man and his joy of painting
made me believe that if you try, anything can be achieved,
you just need to have a go and practice.
Ending with 'thank you for joining me and God bless'
I felt that things might eventually be alright.

Jo Roberts

Open eyes

Time is not a commodity you can store.
Seconds, minutes, hours, all have a use by date
portioned into task and tedium of daily life.
But now I have time to sit,
wrapped in the peppery, clove scent of Sweet Williams.
Time to watch a bee burrow in foxglove flowers,
sounds of their labour amplified by each pink trumpet.
Time to think, take stock of what I do have,
time to relish the sharp stripes of shadow,
time to enjoy a rippling canopy of green against
a freshly washed sky.
Time to enjoy the garden as it stretches in morning light
then sinks contentedly into evening.
It was always here in the background of life,
but now time has given it centre stage.

Jo Roberts

I write plays and have won the Sir Alan Ayckbourn Award for a ten minute play twice, and had a couple performed both locally and beyond. I have a couple of novels and short stories on the go and since 2014 have run a writer's *group in Coventry – that's when I'm not gardening, taking photographs or doing a slot on BBC local radio!*

Jesus in the Time of Covid-19

The cabinet, in panic, were grasping for straws –
they dreamt, in vain, of weekly applause.
Instead, faced a poll-rating nightmare of dread:
spiralling numbers of stubbornly dead.
But what could they do, to quell rising fears?
The public school fools were bereft of ideas.

Then a junior minister piped up and said:
'I've heard of this Jesus, who can bring back the dead!
Let's widen our team, get him on board,
and if it works out, we'll make him a lord!'
So the word went about, and Jesus was found –
for He'd snuck back to earth, second time round.

The PM babbled *'Lazarus!'* wished for more of the same;
slyly made mention of riches and fame.
Jesus was reluctant, but finally said yes
to help all humanity out of its mess.
They stuck Him with the sickest, toiling for free,
no rest, no sleep, and no PPE.

Infected by the virus, in a week He expired,
a spokesperson stormed: *'He's no good – he's fired!'*
And, not for the first time, Jesus ascended;
followers on Twitter were outraged, offended.
Weary, disillusioned, He complained to His dad:
'After 2,000 years, they're still just as bad!'

Martin Brown
Recently retired, all plans blown out the window by the pandemic.

Kept sane during lockdown by streaming theatre performances (thank you, National Theatre, Hampstead Theatre, Globe, RSC!) and by cycling out into nearby countryside for my hour a day exercise (quiet, mostly deserted roads – lovely!) Missed the grandchildren and was especially outraged by Dominic Cummings jaunting round the country at no penalty whilst I couldn't see my newest born.

Pause

You stand at your windows and doors
sharing applause
but I ask you to stop, pause.

Why have you not seen us before?
is this what it takes; to appreciate
what has always been there?
Has Covid-19 made you care?

I will not bask in this applause.
For me it is a bitter pill to swallow...
at first the sentiment brought a tear to my eye
but week on week, it's feeling hollow.

It's too little, too late
to stand and appreciate
after frozen pay,
not enough hours in the day,
over-worked, underpaid –
nursing the neglected trade.

Bursaries ceased,
recruitment and retention decreased,
undervalued as a profession...
well here is my confession.

I am not a hero, nor do I wish to be.
I am a nurse, a wife, a mother, a student...
that is me.

I am not 'at battle' nor am I on the 'frontline.'
These are metaphors for war, not mine.
I am simply doing my job, doing what I'm trained to do –
yes, of course it's riskier, but it's what we signed up to.
But I did not sign up for half measures on safety
or limited PPE...
I fell ill with query Covid, but there was no swab for me.

So please, when you are out at your windows and doors
I ask you to stop, to pause.
We do not need your applause.

We need to be valued, every day...
rewarded with appropriate pay.
Student nurses need their bursaries
the beautiful beast that is the NHS
needs the government to invest –
fill our wards with doctors and nurses,
increase funding to mental health and social services.

Never forget how lucky we are
to have such an amazing health service –
just imagine how great it could be
if we just stopped this lip service.

Charlotte Potter

I am a trainee advanced clinical practitioner currently working in acute care at Warwick hospital whilst doing a part time MSc at Coventry University. I am married with a beautiful five year old girl, and we have recently moved to Bishops Itchington.

It Is OK To Share Your Concerns [1]

All parking is free for the duration of the crisis,
at the parallel universe hospital: extra-galactic, alien, novel.
Inserted by cosmic catastrophe, I shudder into this counterpart earth.
I'm sidestepped through a wriggling wormhole
into a hostile timestream, shielded by waning, waxing invisibility.

Singletons, anonymous in home-made scrubs scuttle past,
unspeaking, crablike. Priests and Levites passing on the other side.
Their backs melting into the wipe-clean walls. Against my wall,
desquamated skin-flakes, electrostatic fragments, clang soundlessly,
clinging stealthily between my shoulders.

Scrubs with the sidewise eyes, of flounders, migrating into adult-ness
contrive to not see me. Others nod-thank me for my restraint:
That I don't claw their exposed forearms for comfort.
That I too pass by on the other side.

In the dead-end corridor, the clatter of weeks-old footsteps echo eerily.
STAFF ONLY signs defend each turning.

In the labyrinth, which way is out, which way the Minotaur?

1: extract from Govt. advice to those shielding:https://www.gov.uk/government/publications/guidance-on-shielding-and-protecting-extremely-vulnerable-persons-from-covid-19/guidance-on-shielding-and-protecting-extremely-vulnerable-persons-from-covid-19 30/5/20

Julia Wallis

I share a home with Bertie, the miniature dachshund, and three spinning wheels, but I've never pricked a finger. Textile working feeds a fertile imagination. Poetry and nature writing come easiest, although I turn my hand to most excuses to put the right words in the right order to paint a picture.

Copsewood Grange House *(A Coventry eulogy)*

The grand old lady of Binley Road
stares blindly out with shuttered eyes
her hair a mass of tumbled vines,
gnarled fingers reaching to the skies.

Born a hundred years ago
she now lies empty, dark and cold
her life of finery is gone,
she never thought that she'd grow old.

As a girl, she was beautiful –
created for a man of wealth.
Clad in the best Italian style,
the years crept by with growing stealth.

As a woman she was powerful –
slender, sturdy, strong and tall.
Families sheltered in her bosom
lives won and lost within her walls.

The decades passed, she saw it all –
watched as the city's life unfolded.
Before her eyes it boomed and bust,
rebuilt after bombs exploded.

The latest threat leaves her nonplussed.
Plague attacks, steals hope and breath...
she knows the city will recover,
but she cannot begin afresh.

The disease has given brief respite,
rush hour silent as a tomb,
workmen forced to down their tools –
all too soon they will resume.

Still and silent, eyes downcast,
she'll soon be destroyed forever –
replaced by younger, sleeker models,
but newer isn't always better.

Annette Kinsella

I have two children aged eight and fourteen, and I entered my poem to help inspire them to write. Three things about me – I am a bookaholic, a former Coventry Telegraph journalist and a former primary school teacher, but now I work for the Department of Education.

Down Our Street

Roshan and Aisha make lots of cups of tea, stick to new daily routines created to maintain cheer. They stare out of the window. They want chocolate bars which they are too scared to go and buy.

Josh, who never had the courage to leave the computer job he hates, and has always longed for an alternative lifestyle, has dug up his small back garden and plants spinach and garlic to bolster his immune system.

Wojcek is desperate to get back to Poland, to see his family, but is worried that if he gets there he will never be allowed to return. He drinks four cans of strong lager, starting at six, every evening.

Liz weaves bright new futures in her mind, of a world that has learnt its lessons, and looks forward to the autumn. She sews scrub bags for the NHS, plans to make recycled masks, knit rainbows.

Jade can't get her usual supply of methadone, but has found some cheap spice. She likes the sunshine. Although she is hungry, she's got the gang, and her lockdown is flying by.

Stephen, aged 75, cupboards overflowing with cheese, ready meals and whisky, thinks it is Xmas. He Facetimes his son every evening at half past six. Eats and drinks like there is no tomorrow.

Lorraine spends ten hours a day on Facebook campaigning for the cure of Covid-19 by a combination of turmeric teas and yogic breathing.

Rob develops business plans for using the last reserves from his bankrupt cafe business, and some thin Government support, for a start-up in developing video games – his teenage passion. He is in discussions with his landlord about unpaid rent.

Chris and Kerri lie in bed every morning, rowing over how much screen time Ben and Gemma, aged eight and six, should have every day. Ben and Gemma are downstairs creating alternative worlds in Minecraft.

Alexandra texts Gilly that a G and T at five tonight in the back garden, with six feet between them, will be completely fine, surely darling.

John is alone in his flat, sweating in bed, waiting for his twice-weekly call from an NHS volunteer telephone befriender.

Louisa bleaches the front letter box, the front door bell, the wing mirrors of her Citroen Picasso, every morning at 7am.

Rashida has spent two days weeping for her Mum, who died aged 52, for lack of PPE. Rashida is also a nurse, goes back to work tomorrow.

Mike eats Monster Munch and reads online conspiracy theories and analysis that show that Covid-19 is a statistical myth created by capitalists to increase global control over consumer populations.

Melanie, asthmatic, wakes up thinking she has Covid every morning. She spends her days on Facebook looking for posts that will offer her lifelines for her more precarious than ever mental health.

Jane is on 80% furlough, and now she can no longer go to restaurants or on holiday, is better off than when she was working. She reads, rings friends, listens to Guardian recommended Spotify lists. She loves lockdown, but knows it is not right to say it.

Ashley clings to the wreckage of S.S. Hope, stares across the grey, choppy sea.

Unwittingly, and despite best efforts, the small corner shop spreads Covid-19.

The pub is closed.

The pigeons coo-coo, coo-coo.

Callum, aged four, draws pictures of giants every day. He loves his mum and dad at home together for this spring that seems to last forever.

Matt Black

The Mad Hermit Poems

#Day 4
Confused, he bleaches his face,
burns the post. All shopping goes
under the stairs for fourteen days, just in case
the baked beans or the J-cloths have it.
He only listens to Radio 4 Extra,
thinks the virus is being spread
by the Goon Show's Dreaded Batter Pudding Hurler,
will eventually be defeated by
Simon Templar as The Saint.

#Day 9
He has a tickly cough all week,
lives on the brink, rides nightmares
into stormy seas of imaginary
sweats. He puts a Post-It note on the fridge –
auto-suggestion is not a route of infection.
Touches nothing, puts garlic up his nostrils.
Runs in circles like Billy the Whizz,
tries to get six feet from himself.
On Friday his cough goes away.

Day 12
Every cough is the beginning,
every temperature rise, each morning shower
starts a road downhill to held-in panic.
He is living an episode
of Get Me Out of the Jungle
or a global version of Casualty.

He would rather have been in Lewis.
At least there would have been good cars,
and his own room in a quiet hospital.

#Day 16
He gets drunk in the afternoon, hopes
he might get used to the new normal,
creativity and charity preferred to clarity
or organisation in Lockdown Fluffyland U.K.
Inspired by plague engravings he googles
origami for eight year olds, Toucan Beak mask.
Wears his red and yellow PPE
on his daily walk in the park,
still holds his breath when joggers spin past.

Day 21
Tired of staying cheerful and Joe Wicks,
he reshapes his childhood into a parade
of striding topiary giants, mother, father,
Thor, Mowgli, Stig the stick-boy
become a walking furnace. He throws
darts at recent death statistics.
Rips up poems into black and white confetti
to set free from the bedroom window
at 8.03pm next Thursday.

#Day 24
He thinks he has contributed
to the national interest

when he joins the long queue
outside Waitrose
wearing a T-shirt that reads:
haiku
twenty thousand deaths
and I worry that I might
run out of olives

#Day 26
He hates the bloody joggers,
leaving spittle in their slipstream,
training to be the clean-lunged Ubermensch.
Dreads the end of lockdown when
Fluffyland becomes Superfluffyland 2.0.
In a pink frock, dressed as Claire of Grayson Perry,
he paints one picture, sixteen portraits
entitled: Family Gatherings Were Found
To Be Far Easier On Zoom.

#Day 29
3am in the kitchen, and sleepless
with statistics, once again he sees
his first world luck has dipped. All change,
no cornflakes, his once precious life now cheap.
His fear buttons get pressed every day.
He repeats, repeats the clichés yet again –
enjoy the sun bla bla, be thankful, keep breathing.
They help a bit, but mostly he gets pissed,
waves his arms and legs to Dancing Queen.

#Day32
He wants to make peace with everything
just in case, prepare the right mantra
to take with him under the ventilator,
like a lifeboat, to help the waves
Let go, let go, let go.
The mantra might be Om, or Please Not This.
He prays for blazing rays of light and love,
expects the usual muddle, struggle,
will hang on to his Abba playlist.

#Day36
He looks – again – for hope inside the fridge.
There's half a bar of Cadbury's Fruit and Nut.
Exhausted by fear, and all the daily questions,
sips tea at the kitchen table, snaps chocolate
into tidy squares, names them – Keep On Worrying,
Dig Deep, Lighten Up, You Never Know.
He laughs, looks into his cup. Dark brown tea
bursts into skies of light – he is stardust,
he is a moment, a pigeon in mid-flight.

Matt Black

I live in Leamington Spa and write for adults and children. I'm a joyful mischief maker, a serious entertainer, a reluctant grown-up and a celebrationist. I was Derbyshire Poet Laureate (2011-2013), my play The Storm Officer toured in 2020 and my next publication is Sniffing Lamp-posts by Moonlight (Upside Down, 2020) a collection of poems inspired by dogs, based on my one-man show The Snoopy Question. www.matt-black.co.uk

Remember

Our
lives have
changed
drastically.
No school, no work.
no flour, no toilet rolls!

We were stuck in our houses
reliant on the news...
nothing could cure
our lockdown blues.

Rainbows were drawn
and pans were hit.
We came together
with united enthusiasm.

As rules were eased,
opportunities were seized
to go out for our daily exercise.

There were some positives,
for the environment,
for climate change...
but soon things returned
to how they had been before.

So, remember these times,
this moment in history.
Remember our key workers
and our community spirit.

Nurture these positive seeds
that have been sown,
and remember...
you are not alone.

Sophia Dore, age 13

I am in Year 8 at Bishop Ullathorne. I have a few unusual interests, like playing the viola and looking after my pet rats, Maple and Pip, and I love horse-riding, baking and losing myself in a good book!

When all this is over

When all this is over,
the world won't be the same –
it's cracked the fabric of our life
with only ourselves to blame.

We stripped the earth's resources
through constant want and need
and could not bring ourselves to share
fruits of insatiable greed.

So nature now puts up a fight,
without discerning care,
hurts enemies and loved ones...
you say, 'It's just not fair'.

But it just wasn't fair
when we cut down the trees
with no home for the songbird
to call on the breeze.

It just wasn't fair
when we laid down new roads
destroying all the habitats
of frogs and newts and toads.

So when all this is over
will we revert to norm?
As those superior beings
Who always scoff and scorn

at all the other species
of the world in which we share?
Do we plan to pay more heed?
Or will we just not care?

Caring is in our nature
and so is self-preserve.
Let's hope when this is over
we get what we deserve.

Cathy Humphrey
I've lived in Coventry for over 20 years and work in marketing for a local college. I have two teenage children and love the great outdoors.

Into Isolation

It was during 5th period that Elijah's life as he knew it would change. His school announced without warning that Year 7 were not to come to school the next day – the school would be closing. 'What, really, Sir? No joke?' Elijah said, meaning to think, but it came out loud.

He was so happy, and all his friends were too. They would be working at home, no school. Whoop! They were so glad that the school would be closing down that they all started screaming and shouting. Little did Elijah know how hard it was going to be.

After school, he had to walk down the road to the primary school where his mum taught.

Unfortunately for Elijah, home schooling did not begin the next day as he had hoped – his bubble was burst. It turned out he was going back to primary school after less than two terms at secondary! His mum was a teacher there, and with his step-dad working and no family able to look after him, primary school it was. He spent the first days of isolation helping in Year 4! By Friday afternoon though, this was to change too…

When Monday came around, the alarm went off – thankfully – an hour later than usual – his new school opened. They set up the new classroom, otherwise known as the dining room, and began logging in to the school work. Elijah's little sister had a weekly chart of work, so she planned out her whole week, but Elijah's work came through everyday… piles of it!

Their new routine had begun, the 'new normal.'

Elijah grew to prefer quarantine. It seemed so much easier – do the work and be free! Well, locked in the house, but free to do what he wanted. The new routine was far better than any school routine – not having to wear a uniform and carry his heavy bag around, especially on PE day. Elijah even found he was sleeping better. Sometimes the work was too hard, but he was lucky to be able to get one-to-one help from his mum. She sometimes became an angry, grumpy teacher with no patience, but still. His uncle and godmother were science teachers, so there was usually someone who could help when he got stuck.

He moaned to his sister regularly. 'I swear I'm getting more lessons than I would in actual school.' That made his mum find extra work for his sister, which made Elijah happier. Win!

When the work was done, he sometimes helped with chores and gardening. They set up a vegetable patch with everything growing in the sunshine, and he liked to water it in the evenings. His uncle ordered him a new seat for his bike, so sometimes he would go bike riding if it got too hot or stressful. The quarantine time seemed to have brought the sunshine out, so they even put the pool up. The water was freezing though, cold as ice and would turn your toes as blue as the sky! Elijah begged for the hot tap hose to be used to fill it up.

Elijah's afternoons were spent riding his bike on the government issued daily exercise allowance. Living by an old golf course had its advantages – he had even found a secret lake with nine ducklings and three moorhen chicks to feed! Then he'd head for home and play on his Xbox or PC. This was the part of the day when he got to talk to his friends and have a laugh and joke, and evenings were usually spent watching movies or playing board games like Monopoly. They even had a family quiz on video chat, but only won once.

Elijah looked around his dining room classroom and realised he was going to miss isolation, when the time came to go back to school – just certain things, like not having to wear that annoying uniform or carry the bag round and trek from class to class to class. All that rushing around had not been fun, and lockdown had been a chance to stop the clock.

But for now, Elijah could only guess when the return might happen…

Kymani-Elijah Cruz, age 11

I play rugby and basketball, and I LOVE gaming and reading about history.

Lockdown Diary

If we'd known 2020 was going to be like this, 2019 could have held on a little longer. It was like someone had clicked their fingers and our universe had switched to another dimension nobody knew about...

Week 1

Whilst you are in your homes, on the streets or in the shops for a pint of milk, be careful because as you turn around there may be a film crew making a documentary on the pandemic. The virus was hugging people, and we no longer could. Children now worked at their dining table at home, parents became qualified teachers and houses were not homes anymore, just the walls keeping us from the hugging motion sweeping through our nation. The virus grew, lives were already lost.

Week 2

Seconds felt like hours, hours felt like months and days felt like years. The time and date had blurred into a distant memory of what was no longer there. We were all living in a history lesson for the next generation. No one could know how bad it is until death comes knocking onto their loved one's door. When you were out to go shopping, the windows were filled with pastel stained rainbows to represent the glimpses of hope people still had.

Week 3

A new week of schooling and concern. At the dreaded time of 6:00pm, you could hear the echoing sound of the news theme song running across the street. The first three weeks in lockdown they couldn't give us answers. Nobody knew anything, but the seven words were a tattoo in your mind. STAY HOME; SAVE LIVES; PROTECT THE NHS. Those seven words were like when you first learnt a nursery rhyme when you were younger, and you can't get it out of your head... yet in nursery, I had no memory of a nursery rhyme meaning suffering. Friends were missed, families were separated, and we were still unsure of what, how and when this hugging virus would stop. Or if it would stop.

Week 5

It was like someone had hit a pause on our whole life but still we were going full speed. No one laughed or was happy anymore. It was as if someone had painted a smile on everyone's face, but once the paint dried and cracked off, people's true faces of shock and concern appeared. Their true feelings were smeared and varnished through their skin, and nothing could change that. The virus had a domino effect and targeted the elderly and people with underlying health issues. You or I could have it right now but not know, and the domino effect could carry on until the trail stopped... but who knew who might be the last to be hugged? A virus is defined as an infective agent that is too small to be seen and can multiply. Whatever we are living in right now was not that; the virus was an uncontrollable monster, and we were in another universe.

Week 7

When everyone heard about the first hug, it was a death threat to everyone. Now it felt normal. It had come to the point where you felt so stressed that every time you woke up you felt like you may have taken your last breath. Our life was the last chapter and 2020 was a devil hanging over us, turning the next page to reveal what was going to hit us in the face. Everyday there was a new story, another thousand hugs wrapped around bodies that didn't deserve to be embraced. Was this our normal or our nightmare?

Present day

Thursday the 4th June at 3:00pm. We are on a film set. I may be saying cut now to end the story, but that doesn't mean our reality of hugging is over. Everyone is used to this new life, but when will it end? On January 1st 2020 we were excited for this new era to begin but now all we ever want is for it to stop. Protect yourselves, stay home, that is how we will end it together. Clutch. Clasp. Hug is our future until further notice. 5... 4... 3... 2... 1... CUT.

Niamh Walsh, age 14

I am in Year Nine at Bishop Ullathorne School.

Cooper

April: four locked doors and a woman
who doesn't know my last name.

We keep our distance, keep to our own time,
soaking into new routines like moonshine in oak.
We leave gifts – a bottle of scented bleach,
a sterilised surface.
We will leave a room if the other enters.

I will wake at 3am
to the whisper of slippers on polypropylene,
an open window swallowing the night.

I will wake with the weight
of needing to be anywhere else.

Hollow barrels sound the loudest.
They don't sink.

I haven't been touched for five weeks.

Jack Cooper
I'm a member of Coventry Stanza and have been published by Young Poets Network, Poetry Birmingham and Under the Radar.
I'm undertaking a PhD in embryonic cell migration at the University of Warwick, and can often be found on Twitter @JackCooper666

Covid-19 Love Poem

Locked down in this place with only you,
no one else to speak to, just us two.

You like your own space and I like mine
and when we ask how we are, we always say, 'fine.'

This little flat feels smaller each hour –
we're confined here like a princess in her tower.

Sometimes tension and bickers happen a lot,
but this just reminds me how lucky I got,

to love a man who is patient and kind,
and likes to hear every little thing on my mind.

Through our worries and fears and long sleepless nights,
you hold me close, tell me it'll all be all right.

Looking to our wedding, set for next June,
at least no one can say that we did it 'too soon.'

If we can get through this lockdown, staying as one,
the rest of our lives should be nothing but fun.

Caileigh McCracken

I'm 24 and work at Severn Trent Water – I moved to Coventry in 2015 for university and loved it so much I never left! I live with my fiancé Tom, the subject of the poem – we met at university and are getting married in June 2021.

Anxious Times

Have you sprayed the toilet flush?
Have you checked your hands are washed?
OK, how many are you meeting?
You're joking – FOUR? Arranged by tweeting!

You've no regard for me, who's shielding,
nightmare, these rules are bewildering!
Protection and safety count in this building.
Rules are rules! No point in gilding!

I know it's hard for my sons confined,
but rules are changing, now refined.
They're really chomping at the bit
to get out there, socialise and mix!

Many challenges I must pursue
checking one son has cleaned the loo –
around the house in everyone's way
are tins of Dettol All-In-One spray.

If I didn't have OCD before the lockdown,
I'm feeling paranoid and quite bogged down.
At this moment in time paranoia is rife
I'm weary of this disease dictating my life!

My mind is anxious, I've no control
I want to escape, to find a loophole!
Son shouts, 'The government have got to your head!'
I shout back, 'Just stay at home instead!

To a certain point I suppose I agree,
but the letter in the post says I'm vulnerable you see!
The stress this lockdown has brought at times
I'm surprised I haven't been driven to crime!

As the lockdown begins to change and evolve
I find I have still more worries to solve.
If I lived on my own I'd feel more secure,
my sons want to venture, new rules are the lure!

Things have calmed down, and that's a start…
I can't help worry for my arrhythmia heart.
Going out masks and gloves are worn,
No more sharing fags, my boys have sworn!

They have missed so much what with uni and work –
how can they be free when Covid lurks?
The R rate decreases day on day…
I wish this virus would go away.

Ange Keen

I am a teacher of art, textiles, food and design technology and have a passion for art, acting and writing. I am an amateur actor for a local theatre, with aspirations to take this further.

What Sort of World?

When this war that now is raging
against an unseen enemy,
finally reaches its conclusion
what sort of world will it be?

When the caretakers can all go home
and can hug their families tight,
can you hold your head up?
Say, 'I helped them win the fight?'

When family after family
stop to count the cost,
we will all grieve together
over loved ones we have lost.

Those that only sit at home
will help bring this to an end,
they can't hug their loved ones,
help to comfort a grieving friend.

So, please do not dismiss this
thinking it can't happen to you,
because the day may soon arrive
when you lose someone too.

Vicki Homan

What Did You Do?

In years to come when young ones ask
'During the virus, what did you do?'
I'll tell them I sat in comfort for a month or two.

While others put their lives at risk,
I sat at home in a comfy chair.
While heroes fought a battle
I just stayed right there.

People died in their thousands
I only saw it on the internet,
I didn't venture outside my home
throughout the worldwide threat.

No, I just stayed in comfort,
and slept safely in my bed,
along with millions of others
who were trying to stop the spread.

Vicki Homan

I love drawing and writing poetry, both of these things have helped keep me sane during this pandemic. When I was younger, I worked at John Barry's in Trinity Street as a window dresser, and also worked at the A.E.I. I have a son and two lovely grandchildren.

The World on Hold

On 23rd March 2020, the country was taken to court and sentenced to seclusion.

23rd May 2020 is the present.

It's the four walls and me. The number four seems generous, juxtaposing the zero occupancy. A place I once called home is now my personal prison.

I'm not alone in this. I continue to remind myself that the world is on hold... a pause for prosperity, taught by the tales of turmoil.

'We're in this together.' Then why do I feel so excluded? You could compare the sinister segregation to the rouge red blood cells in a cancerous body.

One's mental, one's physical.

Both lusting to live life for the ticking time they have. It's the irony of illicit internally sustaining the sickness, yet in my place of protection, I feel fallen. A bug crawling inside my head, eating my euphoria away.

My bliss bleeds out, reaching for a plaster to nurse my negativity. These hazards are the hate on my heart, and with this despondence, I've detected my downfall. Tolerant to tangible terror but enervated with emotions.

One outplays the other.

Despite the depression, I've learned so much. A life lesson on how to live. Something I've done for fifteen years, now sterilised as a story. My new chapter feels like a new book, jumping from the jaded to jubilance.

My words walk the world's atmosphere, but that furthers the light at the end of this time-consuming tunnel. The procession of my pessimism opens my edged eyes, an optimism born through the talents of a tragedy. To think that my exultation evolved from a global extermination.

Lives lost to my lucidity.

I know I'm not to blame. No fingers should be pointed... we will bounce back like a boomerang, a trialled triumph.

It can only get better.

Leah Evans, age 15

Corona's Challenge

The truth burnt my ears.

My complexion complemented by my coursing blood, my face full from fear. A hypochondriac hating life as it acts antiquity. Tears of trepidation tripped off my cheeks. Each droplet was my dolour, oozing onto the opaque grounds of the outlawed outdoors. My consciousness was corrupted with a cacophony of conspiracies. This feeling followed my every move.

The norm metamorphosed to mayhem.

The tumult of terror trudged through towns, mutilating masculinity and modifying them to meek men.

All at risk.

We hide in homes as it strips our streets of superheroes who stand their ground for stability in society. We are all held hostage by a transparent terrorist who snatches our loved ones from our own desperate grasp.

It doesn't care who you were before; a criminal, a chaperone. Its merciless manner adds to its ruthless reputation. It targets the weak, preys on people's perception and pilfers them from our world.

Challenging children, attacking our anatomy.

It lingers in our lungs until it chooses to make a name of itself.

Jumping from ship to ship, its spread is undetected as it sails the globe gloating its genocide. Our clips of courage don't compare to the key workers who are destined to defeat the devils drudge. The instinctive idea is survival of the fittest, but the virus continues to break the laws of science.

It covers its tracks and produces new patterns of crime.

It teases teens who already have its malignant movements maltreating their malleable minds.

It indents its insidious intentions into our euphoric expectations. Fictional films become reality as the roles of television are flipped. Despite all dangers, faith is our forward, our freedom.

The ultimate test from the almighty himself.

I pray we pass.

Leah Evans, age 15

My family is literally a cocktail of countries, because nearly every member is from a different place. I enjoy poetry and creative writing and if shopping is a hobby I'll go with that, but I really love travelling too – it's like a legal way to run from reality and live a different life for a fragment of time. My aspirations change almost every day, but at the moment I'd like to become a therapist as I love advising family and friends.

Lockdown Rainshower

It's raining cats and dogs
and warty toads and frogs
and red kneed bats and bowler hats...
it's raining big fat logs.

It's raining needles and pins
and rusty cans and tins
and things I don't like that give me a fright
such as sprouts and wheelie bins!

It's raining apples and pears
and dolls and fluffy brown bears
and muddy pigs in curly wigs...
it's raining plastic chairs.

It's raining bacon and eggs
and washing lines and pegs
and cowboy suits and sour fruits...
it's raining hairy legs.

It's raining forks and rakes
and chocolate bars and cakes
and glasses of milk and colourful silk...
it's raining protein shake.

Zebby Neat, age 9

I live at home with my parents, three brothers and sister. I love sports, especially football and Gaelic football, and I play basketball too. I enjoy writing poems as it's an escape from all the craziness in this house, and my dream is to become a professional sportsman or have my poems published!

Lockdown Life

The virus came from China, of that there's little doubt,
But was it manufactured? How did it come about?

Some think it came from pangolins, from bats or from a lab,
I'm not sure we will ever know, but either way it's bad!

It quickly spread around the world and soon was claiming lives.
Headache, cough, pneumonia – not everyone survives.

The hunt is on to find a cure and halt the virus spread.
If only we could kill it, could somehow stop it dead!

The world has changed forever in ways we've never known.
Half the world is out of work or doing so from home!

All holidays are cancelled and the beaches are all closed
There's fewer cars and buses travelling on our roads.

We now have social distancing and have to keep apart
But some people ignore this rule – I guess they're not too smart!

Pubs and clubs have all shut down and so have all the gyms.
Our social lives have changed so much – now we must stay in!

As this lockdown continues and we're all still stuck at home
Many live with family, but some are all alone.

Computers, phones and video calls all help us keep in touch.
Internet and mobile phones have never been used so much!

So many workers furloughed, but other workers key
We wait to hear what's happening – what will it mean to me?

The press all try to guess what Boris is going to say
Will restrictions now be lifted? Can the kids go out to play?

When will there be a cure for this? When will the lockdown end?
Staying in the house all day drives people round the bend!

A new vaccine is needed which will fight this disease off.
Until that time is on us, beware of every cough!

Stephen Hartopp

I am married with three children, three grandchildren, and another on the way. I served 22 years in the Royal Engineers, living in Germany, Cyprus and throughout the UK, but Coventry has always been home.

Outbreak

In dreams, before daybreak,
I still go to places other
than my home. People die
of things other than the virus;
others gather to grieve them.
Then again, before daybreak,
in dreams, I inhabit other
homes, other selves, break out
of lockdown to do mysterious
things; things psychically, not
physically, essential. Other
than that, in dreams, I receive
touch, but even in those dreams,
there is a barrier, a physical
thing between the other, and my
skin. In dreams, I marry – under
lockdown – as if marrying an
unsuitable other was still an option.
You cannot get married or register
a civil partnership at the moment.
You cannot register a birth, nor
register the reality of a new-
born relative against your skin.
Other than that, you can do
most of the things you would
want to do. You can prepare your
business for Brexit. You can
menstruate. You can roam other
worlds, in dreams, before

daybreak, worlds which look a lot
like the world locked into
memories, only charged with
grief and longing. If by day, you
tell yourself you're OK, that's
OK. But know that other part
of you, the part that wanders
into psychic spaces in dreams
before daybreak, gathers
with others to grieve, inhabits
other homes and selves. Other
than that, do not fail to know
the part of you that breaks
out of lockdown, marries,
registers touch, goes
elsewhere to places, in dreams,
places other than home.

Emma Kemp

I live in Canley, where I run the Coventry Stanza of the Poetry Society, and have had work published in various poetry journals. In my spare time, I practice social work under different guises – part-time for a local authority supporting disabled adults, part-time as a trainer, and part-time offering specialist support to people in chronic pain. I was grateful to have been locked down with my long-suffering housemate, my cat, and my South-facing garden.

Natty's Cure

The world is at war,
unseen enemy,
to our collective biologies,
I can only breathe,
I can only sit under my cherry tree,
daily prayer,
yoga,
nature,
space,
quietude,
then, check on loved ones,
old friends near and far,
offer support,
hear endless corona reports,
search for work,
check the household budget.
Can we survive?
Are the vulnerable protected?
What's the hidden agenda?
Surveillance is upped,
leaders flex their muscles,
patents for cures.
Hear my cure...
don't give fear a place at your table,
open your hearts and minds,
to your own power,
our unity, our hope and
our strength
#staysane

Natty Graña

This life apart

Is not for me –
I need a friendly touch,
I miss a best mate's hug.
This life apart from you is not for me –
I crave beloved's kiss,
that sweet honey's loving I miss,
but even just a brush in a crowd,
a stranger's laugh,
a shared audience appreciation.
This life apart from you all
is too hard to bear,
surreal scenes of empty streets,
as if war made us fearfully retreat.
Family time is a distant memory
from before this time,
a time of connection past.
When we get back together,
long may harmony last!

Natty Graña

I have lived and worked in Coventry on and off since the age of seven, and have brought up my child alone. I consider myself a campaigner, a doer, a healer and a mystic, but down to earth, fun and friendly too!

Where Did All the People Go?

outside wounded cathedral

beyond the walls
where grey slabs
jut from tufty green

I
pause   pause   pause
to absorb
paws   paws   paws

urban squirrel
playing among the dead
oblivious, carefree

except she isn't
she isn't playing
frantic
claws   claws   claws
scrabble for what always came so easy

coachloads on
tours   tours   tours
handfuls of essentials
exchanged for selfies
have spoiled instinct
revealed a symbiosis so fragile

already, our cossetted critters

fade to lean
and wary

natural order
restored   restored   restored

cuteness endangered.

Raef Boylan

Born, matured (sort of) and based in Coventry, I'm a writer whose short stories and poetry explore social realism. I run the monthly poetry night, 'Fire & Dust', edit HCE magazine and have represented Coventry poets as part of the twin cities exchange in Cork, Ireland.

Breathe

It was just an ordinary day. Children's voices ringing out, the hustle and bustle of school life. We were in our safe cocoon. It was scary out there, though – the news headlines flashing before our eyes. Pandemic. What did that mean? Research, let's research, that's what librarians do.

Hmmm. Spanish flu pandemic after WWI. Second wave. Third wave. Gasp – could it be the same for us? The ordinary day became a not so ordinary day. Suddenly no meeting in groups, out in the fresh air, don't congregate in enclosed spaces.

Wash your hands! Hands raw.

Masks.

Social distancing. Steal a hug? No way! Two metres apart at all times.

Tension. Frustration. Fear.

The virus is all around us, hunting, stalking, wearing our resistance down.

Lockdown... we're going into lockdown. Quick, get finished, go home. Grab all the work gear you can as you'll be working from home. Don't come back in! Furlough. What's this? The next step. No work. What do I do now? I've always been so busy. Hub of the school and all that.

Take a breath. Breath – that's the key. Suddenly thousands of people are doing just that, taking their last breaths.

Don't panic, be calm. The fear is rising, it's a thick dark

cloud of menace. Head in hands – breathe.

Look – the sun is shining, it's a beautiful day. Let's venture out. Daily exercise. Hmm, I'm a couch potato with a book in my hand.

Breathe the air. Eyes swoop the landscape. Beauty everywhere. Suddenly I am free again like a butterfly soaring high. Walking. Talking. Sharing.

Into this scary place comes hope. I will grab it now with both hands and walk. Going forward.

The future is out there. Who knows what it holds? I breathe the air, close my eyes, open them again and walk …

Julie Needham

I'm a Coventry kid through and through and have always had a passion for both reading and writing – I was a librarian for many years. I have three children and two grandchildren, enjoy travelling with my husband around the UK and have a strong Christian faith.

Coronavirus Storm

Lockdown, lockdown, how you came like a tornado
storming the calm world!
Well, no school, no friends or family to see
or places to be.
I feel overwhelmed
and read and read to try and understand.
Masks, masks and gloves everywhere!
I'm aghast at the news,
death and sadness ensue.
Coronavirus swamps the earth
like a tangled spider's web.
I become a teacher
and homeschooling becomes the norm.
I juggle the balls like a clumsy clown.
No cars, planes or humans in sight.
An eerie, post-apocalyptic silence descends.
But then, like all species, we adapt and unite.
I embrace this simple life,
reading, drawing, cooking and gardening.
I care for and nurture my plants, watching them grow and grow.
The garden becomes my sanctuary for hope.
I feel tranquil and free to be me.

Soufia Arif

I live with my husband and two daughters. I have worked in university libraries and in Careers. I love cheese, gardening and film noir.

Ockdoon

Firstly, let me introduce myself. My given name is Sherbert – I am what you humans call a cat, and I share my house with my three human servants. 'Strong One' is so called because he is next in line to me, my deputy if you will. I respect him to a degree but know that I am undoubtedly in control. 'Weak One' is the lowest of the three, and will do whatever I ask of her. 'Small, Noisy One' is the hardest to figure out. He hasn't always been here and at first he was no bother, but as the years have passed he has grown and changed. I have little control over him and fear that he could easily usurp me and claim my throne. Luckily, he spends vast amounts of time away from my domain.

Until recently, that is…

It all started a few months ago. The big humans started acting strangely. They appeared on edge and kept whispering about something called 'Ockdoon'… they even had the audacity to ignore me when I ordered them to give me food. When 'Small, Noisy One' walked into the room they stopped whispering and became all fake jolly, talking about different things. It was very odd, particularly as 'Small, Noisy One' shouldn't even have been there.

Not on a Monday!

Over the next week or so, things got worse. 'Small, Noisy One' was still at home, and annoyingly so were the other two. No-one seemed to go anywhere. They were just… there. All the time. Of course, I exaggerate slightly as 'Strong One' did go out sometimes and he must have been going somewhere very important as there was a big song and dance every time he went out and even more fuss when he came back. Lots of washing hands and spraying him with stuff out of a can. He came back with food-based presents for all of us and he took to wearing weird things on his hands and hiding his face a lot.

Luckily, that first day when I felt ignored was just a glitch. It seemed that the humans revered me even more than before, because every time they saw me they put food into my dish. I noticed that it wasn't just me that was being fed more often… whenever I wandered through my kitchen, one of them was always there, looking for some sort of titbit in the cupboards or fridge. The most unusual thing was the oven, normally only switched on once a day. It now seemed to be in almost constant use, churning out cakes and biscuits which the humans devoured in seconds. We were all getting significantly wider.

I wasn't the only one to notice the expanding waistlines. The big humans decided to combat this by jumping around in front of the TV whilst puffing a lot. 'Small, Noisy One' preferred to play in the garden but annoyingly he also tried to include me in his antics. Whenever I retreated to one of my favoured sleeping places, he found me and chased me out. It was fun at first, but soon became wearing, especially as the weather got hotter and hotter. Sometimes I wished 'Strong One' could take off my fur like he did to 'Small, Noisy One,' using the weird buzzing things he called clippers. It looked a bit odd for a while but certainly cooler.

I noticed people didn't visit anymore. I didn't mind this, although I did miss the extra treats that I used to get when the older humans came over. Sometimes I swear I could hear other people somewhere in the house, but when I checked, all I could find was 'Small, Noisy One' talking to one of his screens. Very strange.

As the weeks passed, the humans became less distracted and more purposeful. They still had weird moods but they seemed to laugh and play together more than I had ever seen them do before. New things started to appear in the house and garden – a vegetable plot, a freshly painted chest of drawers, pictures hung on walls. Sheds were tidied and boxes sorted. It was fascinating. 'Weak One' spent ages making a blanket thing out of scraps of material. It looked quite comfy when she'd finished and I was quite put out when she gave it to 'Small, Noisy One' for his bed.

The humans often sat at the table together doing something they called home school. At first this normally ended up with one or all of them storming off, but after a while they began to enjoy it. I began to settle into the pace, discovering new hidey holes and learning to tolerate the humans.

There was one thing that I couldn't understand – every now and again the humans would jump up and shout 'eight o'clock!' for no reason whatsoever. They would rush to open the windows and start bashing things together, shouting like crazy people. They weren't the only ones either. I could hear them all outside. Luckily it didn't last long and afterwards my humans would just sit back down as though nothing had happened.

They really are a peculiar species.

Yesterday, my humans went out.

No warning, nothing. They went out all day and didn't come back until evening. I really don't get it, I was just getting used to them all being around all the time and now it seems that it's all changing again. Mind you, I can't pretend I don't enjoy having the house to myself...

Amanda Kirbyshire

I live in Coventry with my husband, nine year old son and, of course, Sherbert the cat. At some point in the dim and distant past I was a scientist but now I am enjoying my new found love of creative writing!

Change in a blink of an eye...

A brilliant world plunged into darkness, and now this has opened a gateway for racism, hate crime and verbal abuse. Because of Covid-19, a lot of people with mental health issues are stuck at home, and for me, that's been weird. It feels like I'm stuck in my own head. So, I sleep... to just... dream...

Floating in there with all of these thoughts.

'Heyyy, we aren't just thoughts!' whined Schizophrenia.

'I have thoughts... wouldn't like to share them though,' mumbled Depression as she gazed into space with a blank look on her face.

Oh my gosh, guys, I almost forgot to introduce you to... well ... I guess they're... basically other people's emotions. All of the emotions in our world. In quarantine, they're the only friends I've got, so I like to talk to them and humanise them because... well... I'm lonely.

'Oh h-h-ii Tracey, how are you today?' stuttered Anxiety as he rushed to the nearest chair and bounced his leg up and down, his face wrinkled with worry.

'Um... I guess I'm OK, how you are, Anxiet-'

'What are you doing, Anxiety? You're irritating me with your... leg... and you know how I don't like people being out of line!' OCD interrupted, the words tumbling out without him even thinking.

'OMG, that is so sad! You know what else is sad? How I'm so blooming hungry!' complained Bulimia. The room vibrated as her stomach rumbled.

''Wait,' I cut in. 'Can you guys hear that?'

In the distance, I heard a loud booming sound. At first, I thought it was Bulimia's tummy but then I caught a glimpse of the sky outside. I. Was. TERRIFIED. The clouds were fiery red, the sky looked like it was bleeding... it was like the end of the world.

Immediately, I ran downstairs and yanked open the door to reveal an isolated outside. I took a few steps more and saw cars on fire, buildings demolished. Suddenly, I saw a woman coughing, limping my way. In fear, I took a few steps back.

'Please, help me! I've got the virus!' she pleaded.

I blinked. 'What happened? To the country? To our world?'

'Oh, you don't know?' she scoffed. 'Coronavirus RUINED our world. 99.9% of the population, gone.'

'No, no... that can't be possible!'

'Oh, believe it. Nature has won.'

At that moment, as if on cue, the rumbling sound increased in volume and power.

The sick woman looked afraid. 'She is coming for us. Child, you must hide!' she whispered.

'Why, what will 'she' do?!'

'Let's just say if she catches you, you and your ancestors will meet again,' the woman explained.

'Wow – this is depressing!' called out Depression, still clutching onto the walls above the threshold for dear life.

'Tracey, are you OK out there?' shouted Anxiety, with fear taking over his voice.

'Oh... I forgot the emotions! They are still at the house, can they come with us?' I asked.

'Fine, but if they make a sound, they're all roadkill,' said the lady.

'Come on guys,' I whispered. 'But be quiet! May I ask your name?'

'Chikere, but you can call me Chik...' The woman reached out for my hand, then pulled back abruptly. 'No, we can't make contact, the coronavirus is HIGHLY contagious. Keep your distance'.

'Fine by me, Chik,' I agreed.

After walking a few miles, Chikere constantly coughing and OCD moaning every two minutes, we settled down and found a place to rest.

'Schizophrenia, did you take your medicine?' questioned OCD.

'Yes... OK... fine, no! Only because I thought the bottle was possessed...'

'Wait guys, shush... I think someone is watching us!'

The wind whistled as it blew past all of us with such force that it sent us tumbling over.

'Who's there?' Anxiety called out.

'Not who, what!' a voice behind us bellowed, and Chik turned around with a gasp.

'You! What... what do you want, Nature?' she whimpered.

'To rid this earth of you all!' the voice boomed. 'You were the ones who put plastic in my oceans. You treated my lands like dirt, you never appreciated me. As payback I created the Coronavirus, to wipe out the human race... but the virus isn't finishing you off quickly enough. Let me speed up the process!'

Nature loomed down towards Chik with the intention of killing her.

'NO!' I cried out, trying to protect my friend. Nature used all of her power and might to finish me off, her lightning strike creating a scar on my back that would last on my skin forever.

With a huge breath, I woke up and sat up on my bed, drenched in sweat.

'Wait... it was just a dream!' I mumbled to myself.

I jumped up and gazed out of the window. I saw clear sky, but in doing so I glanced in the mirror and caught a glimpse of my lower back and saw the scar Nature had given me.

'It was a dream, right? Or was it…?'

Tracey William, age 13

I think that mental health is important, and that it should be recognised more – so I made a story up based on a dream I had that humanised mental health illnesses themselves, with a fun and relatable storyline!

| |

Pause.
Life for the past seven weeks.
Pause.
The space from one straight solid line to a parallel other.
Pause.
The state of mind in between one state of life to an unknown next.
Pause.
An uncertain, unsettling void lived simply day by day.

Pause.
It ain't no holiday.
Yes it's respite from the daily commute,
endless coffee and relatively trivial inconveniences.
Yes there's no immediate anxiety
of the virus swimming
in or around me in these four walls.
But we're no life savers,
key service deliverers or world savers,
no purpose other than to sit, run, scoff.
Live and let live. Literally.

A pause for some.
A wide open space, ironic in lockdown.
Space for thought, argument, anxiety, silence.
Thinking, running and pointless eating.

A pause.
For some a state of privilege.
For some a living nightmare.
For some a new temporary normal.

A pause of sorts for others.
No order, orduuuuur.
Instead grappling, squabbling, lobbying.
Governments and all sorts of associations
doing 'something', somewhere.

Pause.
Only the second line now isn't so parallel.
The void widens.
Empty space, empty brain, just no empty belly.
Pause.
Now the pause lengthens
and the 'other side' stands strong, but oh so distant.
We continue to play.

| |

Hannah Green

I am a keen runner, which fuels my love of food and dining, and I also enjoy theatre, comedy and the best of BBC, Netflix and Prime. I work in marketing and communications.

My Lockdown

Lunch club at OLA has to stop...
how I miss all the people that went.
Then on 17th March, empty the food bank
to send the food back to main warehouse.
Had a hair appointment for Thursday
on the Monday got a call
to see if I could go in that day.
My hospital appointment's cancelled,
car MOT cancelled
and not been out since.
Glad to have This Morning and
Loose Women for a good old laugh.
Watching the weeds grow under my car
like the roots of my hair.
Had remote team meetings
Mass by YouTube on Sunday
by Father Emmanuel.
Got to know my son again
(23, still living at home).
Watched the pigeons on the fence
do what they do every year.
Had the letter about five weeks now,
not to go out for twelve weeks...
but then the government said
that we can now go out.
Thank you.

Trish Harper

I moved to Coventry in 1997 from Preston. I'm married with two children, help out at the OLA lunch club and have been a school governor for twelve years. Injuries resulting from a road traffic accident in my past have resulted in the eventual loss of a leg, but I try not to let this stop me!

The Longest Words I've Ever Heard

Sloping shoulders shifting full-on fatigue
from the tired, oxygen marches warlike,
armoured armies administering,

peeking from the mask of injustice,

tight temples, desolate lashes stooping
to attention, no commanding blinks wiping
away worries stamped with solitude

stuffing emotions under seats we sit on,

isolation is inky, do not re-read this chapter
in a cloud covered sky, it will scar our eyes,
furrow our brows rutting deeper with time,

unable to unfold our stiffening collars,

a shouldered barricade from grief; a pithy
pallor painting shuttered doorways, windows
underdressed, shouldering last season's style,

outdated opening hours over the hill,

gale force anxieties contained like a flagon
of fighting fists; we could not see tomorrow
morning would not resemble life as we knew it,

that we would fall to our internal floor,

hands scrunched into white knuckles
of disaster, silent sentences swallowed
inside muzzled mouths searching out air,

stay safe… the longest words I've ever heard.

Laura Smith

While We Can
(staying alert – 2 days prior to lockdown)

Walkies – wet noses shoot from the rug, bright eyes dart,
we can still do this… apparently,
so while we can we will take you both, walk through
damp woody moss; we came across
a clear marsh pool, akin to a mill pond against
the calamity of the world, edging delicately
you licked the surface, would not venture further,
'not a water baby,' yet your best pal
can't wait to feel coolness tickling his tummy,
we can see this deepening his spirit.

Walkies – striding in companionship, each knowing no different,
yet life could soon feel like
a full stop, so while we can we will stride out,
before long we may find ourselves walking
in circular motion across our back gardens to and fro,
green lawns worn down, will we too
become worn down? Will you let out a long howl
pining for lush fields where running is
your purpose? We can see nose and ears twitching
to the smells that evade human senses.

Walkies – babbling gave birth to our ears, this time
on loan for the first time, so while we can
we walked, the path offered up a trophy, round and green,
your outstretched mouth
encircling it with joy; racing to the edge it dropped…

captured by the swirl, eddying, we could
not reach, your paws broke the surface first, you were in,
surprised we turned to see our
'not a water baby' become baptised, once in,
we could see a return visit was your mission.

Walkies – heading downstream ignoring our shouts,
your pal was enraptured, eyeing the escape artist bobbing…
drawing you away; so while we could we scrambled,
scrambled to where you squelched through marshland –
seemingly stuck at one point –
yet freed up making headway back to us,
grabbing your mud clogged harness to freedom,
racing you towards the clear babbling edge,
securely held we doused your weighty coat,
we could see, the brown fade… washed and racing.

Laura Smith

I was born in Coventry to an English mother and an Irish father, and married in my twenties. Qualifying as a Therapeutic Counsellor almost ten years ago has brought many rewarding moments. I am a founding member of Cov Stanza, a monthly poetry group, and a member of the Poetry Society. I like to perform poetry at open mics and other gatherings, and my work has appeared in magazines, anthologies, local newspapers and online.

Behind The Mask

PPE is vital to protect our wonderful NHS staff,
this pandemic forcing the need for gowns, visors, masks.
It's our new uniform style, it's our protective shield,
not all heroes wear capes... these heroes are real.

We deliver our care to the highest standards we can reach,
patients poorly, short of breath, struggling to speak,
they are scared and anxious, wondering what will happen next...
we do our best to comfort them, ease worries and distress.

As we hold their hands and try to diffuse their fear,
behind our visors and masks we sometimes shed a tear.
Our hearts are heavy that their families can't be by their side,
we won't leave them, don't you worry, it's part of our nursing pride.

Behind the masks are so many things you cannot see or hear,
our smiles that frame our faces, our sadness and our fears,
we work tirelessly trying to save as many lives as we can,
doctors, nurses, paramedics, the whole NHS gang.

Amongst this sadness and grief there are happy moments too,
midwives protecting mums and babies that are due,
they are ready and waiting for the contractions to start,
the safe delivery of babies is a magical art.

I'd like to say thank you to ALL of the NHS team,

with hearts so big it makes our care of others a reality not a dream,
my heart beats proudly for the job that we do,
a job that would be impossible without our army in blue.

Ness George

I am a Palliative Care Nurse Specialist at Warwick Hospital and am very proud of the job that I do and the colleagues I work with. I am also a Mum to two amazing kids.

High Tide

I was born in Vancouver, Canada. And although I only lived there when I was quite young, I have always been fascinated by and drawn to the ocean. Whenever I return to Vancouver, I take time to walk along the Seawall in Stanley Park, looking out at English Bay and the Pacific Ocean.

When I was about 12 or 13, my Mum put the three of us kids in a van and we drove across Canada during the summer. I remember being overwhelmed by the Bay of Fundy in Nova Scotia, which apparently has the world's highest tides. The tidal range in the Bay of Fundy is something like 13 metres (or about 43 feet) – which is pretty amazing when compared with the average tidal range worldwide of only about one metre (just over three feet).

If you are present at high tide, the water comes crashing into the funnel shaped bay with great force. Loud and roaring, it bloody well commands your attention. Ignoring the tide or resistance to that natural movement can be fatal.

But at low tide, the Atlantic Ocean is beautiful and calm. It might even invite a quiet moment of reflection, just sitting down with a cuppa (or a pint, if you prefer) and looking out at the ocean.

Perhaps we can all agree that 2020, with its waves aggressively crashing against us for most of the year, has been a year of high tide. COVID hit us, tsunami-like, and forced us to batten down the hatches, forced us into our homes to shelter, forced us to self-isolate, and forced us to stock up on loo roll (never understood that last one). And, sadly, the devastating waters of high tide overtook way too many people, the coronavirus pandemic leading to an overwhelming loss of lives.

But we have been witness to much good as well. I'm sure I'm not the only one who has seen the best in people emerge because of this time. Throughout the pandemic, I've had the pleasure of talking with many people who are searching for something more in their lives. Something that helps us grapple with the importance of our major events – moments of national tragedy, moments of death, moments of birth, times of deep loving, or even times of great beauty like a sunset so beautiful you just have to stop in your tracks to watch it. All those moments, for me at least, damage the fallacy of thinking I'm in complete control of my life and encourage me to grasp towards something bigger than myself. I would define that 'something' as God.

There is a story I once read about a Rabbi during a natural disaster. Someone asked him how on earth he could explain such a tragic act of God. The Rabbi argued that the disaster was just an act of nature. However, the act of God occurred when people stepped up to help each other.

Whether you want to frame it in terms of faith or not, I think we can agree that we have seen so much good throughout this time of tragedy. I, for one, certainly know my neighbours considerably better now than I ever did before. The vast majority of us have risen to the Covid-19 challenge, have recognised how interconnected we are – how I am only because you are, because we are – helping neighbours and volunteering in the community, trying to make a new normal that is bigger, gentler, more inclusive and more caring than the past.

And I also think I'm not the only one who has noticed the waves crashing against the shoreline of our nation and institutions, eroding and wearing the edges away, exposing the dramatic social inequality that was always there in our society. There are clearly urgent matters in our nation that are screaming for our attention. Amid an international pandemic, we are provided with the opportunity to summon up the courage to address systemic racism and sexism, classism and ableism, homophobia and transphobia, prejudice and intolerance towards immigrants and refugees, homelessness, and the list goes on…

This really is a remarkable moment ('unprecedented' really does work better than 'remarkable', but I'm pretty sick of how over-used and cliché the word has become). It is a remarkable moment, a potential tipping point in time, to try to examine the root causes of our disunity as a nation and to work together to find solutions that will help us live well, to have brave conversations that just might lead to healing.

So, buoy up, and a personal thank you to the people of this city of Coventry that we love, for all that you are and all that you do!

P.S. – I know it's very strange to keep using water and ocean imagery when we live in Coventry, a place that's pretty landlocked and fairly far from any ocean. I kept trying to find imagery that was flexible and that would be appropriate for a range of people. 'High tide' seemed better to me than 'dumpster fire of a year' or 'the 2020 sh*tshow', but I guess I'll leave that for you to decide.

Rev. Dwayne Engh

The Reverend Dwayne Engh is proud to serve as vicar of St Mary Magdalen Church in Chapelfields (known locally as 'the church with the blue roof'). In his pre-ordained life, he was blessed with a wide range of opportunities as a composer, conductor, percussionist, drummer and educator.

There's no alarm anymore

There's no alarm anymore.
My day starts when the sound of hungry mews
can no longer be ignored.

My partner still works.
He's a 'hidden hero,'
'feeding the nation'.
I am not these things.
Some days I can barely manage to feed myself;
other days all I do is eat.

Indefinitely.
That's how long I've been furloughed.
At first I had grand ideas:
I'll finally learn to french plait,
I'll sort the garden out,
I'll redecorate.
I haven't done any of those things.

I worry about returning to work,
about having to use the bus again.
I wonder whether they'll let me shout DING
instead of pressing the stop button?

I Zoom three times a week
but I've never felt so still.
I rarely leave the house
but when I do it is cautious, wild-eyed,
zigzagging across roads and flattening myself against walls.

I lie in bed and stare at the darkness,
waiting for sleep to come and find me.
There's no alarm anymore.

Hana Evans

I'm a keen reader, and part of a weekly pub quiz team. I've recently taken up cross stitch to try and fill my time, but am desperate to return to my job as a Wedding and Events Coordinator. I live with my partner Daniel and our three cats, Rogue, Phoenix and Gallifrey.

The Secret Unicorn

Posy was jumping on the trampoline to cheer up.
She was missing school and missing her friends.
She stayed busy baking cakes, gardening and riding her bike.

Huge raindrops fell to the ground.
Pitter patter, pitter patter. 'Oh no,' said Posy.
She could hear angry thunder above.
She ran inside and sat by the log fire.

Suddenly, a sparkly unicorn flew down from the sky
and perched on the table!
Posy rubbed her eyes and thought she was dreaming,
but it was still there.
She hugged the unicorn.
The unicorn flapped its wings
and floated higher and higher
flying away towards the park.

Nuria Afzal, age 4

I am 4 years old and love Peter Rabbit. I have an older sister who is 7.
I love going on holiday and have travelled to Dubai, Doha and Islamabad.
I enjoy riding my bike, going to the beach and baking cakes.

Imagined Recall

I imagine the gathered people at the village hall,
the days of final planning, caterers, flowers.
In no time at all it seems the ship of their
sixty-year marriage had sailed across an open sea.
Who knows what the celebration would mean
to me and others, my sister and brothers.
We went from black and white to colour,
I had the enlargements done, ready to hang.
There would have been a band, but not a loud one,
folks would have been able to hear each other.
And my parents, old and slightly sunken, would sit together,
and the 'greats', who hardly knew them, would
have travelled from Dorset and Worcester
and sat at a table, in an overdressed cluster.
And from the table centres swaying balloons
would romance each other as fifties tunes
curled from the walls, and I would have spoken
to more people than I usually do and glanced
at mum and dad, smiling, bemused, and at their age
I suppose, just a little confused. What a night it
might have been for all who came. They'd take some cake,
and those still awake at the end would clear the foil plates
of lonely vol-au-vents and sausage rolls, that last scoop
of trifle clinging to the bowl. The band would have stopped,
a CD would play, something by Vera Lynn meeting up
on another day. And mum and dad would not even be tired,
just lovingly admired for their diamond bash. All smiles
they'd have been, and at some point they'd have held hands
like young lovers again. All the demands of recall and photos

would have been graciously done, the odd faltering word
would be a brilliance not a blemish on their stunning
resilience to age and all its potholes and tripwires; an example
to which us younger ones might aspire: if we could.
And the night would have passed into another day,
and all the guests, like shadows, would have slipped away
as we cleared up with black bags, scooping up paper, name tags
and bits of nostalgia stuck to the walls.
And mum and dad would return to their home,
tired at last with all that had passed on the night –
and the six decades before. They might have slept
like logs well into the morning, and a new day
would have seen them tiredly aglow, smiling, sipping tea.
But something came, unseen, and stopped it all.
I pretend it actually happened. Above is my imagined recall.

Dave Copson

I teach Creative Writing in Coventry; a city where my grandfather, as an auxiliary fireman, was called upon one November night in 1940 to help put out a bit of a fire in the cathedral! I write poetry, flash fiction, short stories and have written two novels. Apart from writing I enjoy listening to music, playing chess and painting, and have exhibited work at the Royal Academy in London. I am married and have a daughter who is currently training to be a doctor in Cuba.

An Invitation

To have a go... at poetry, prose, art, music,
dance and more – uncover your creative side...

To share... your creative side
and connect with others...

on Facebook: Sitting Rooms of Culture
Instagram: Sitting_Rooms_of_Culture
Twitter: @CultureRooms
TikTok: @sittingroomsofculture

Resources

BBC Poetry – famous poets read their poems
https://www.bbc.co.uk/arts/poetry/outloud/
BBC Poetry Resources – for primary and secondary students
https://www.bbc.co.uk/programmes/articles/5y4773X4mxPhXGTcbHDxN3J/poetry-resources
Poetry Challenges with David Morley. Podcasts
https://warwick.ac.uk/newsandevents/podcasts/media/more/poetrychallenges
Spoken word artists https://applesandsnakes.org/
Writing Challenges with David Morley. Podcasts
https://warwick.ac.uk/newsandevents/podcasts/media/more/writingchallenges/

Developing your writing: local workshops and groups

Coventry Stanza Poetry Group
https://poetrysociety.org.uk/membership/poetry-society-stanzas/
Coventry Writers Group
http://www.cwn.org.uk/arts/coventry-writers-group/index.html
Coventry Young Writers Group (School year 3-6) at the Belgrade Theatre on one Saturday per month
https://writingwestmidlands.org/coventry-young-writers-group
Free monthly poetry workshops with Positive Images. Last Sunday of every month 1pm-3.30pm. Usually at Central Library, but via YouTube since Covid
https://www.youtube.com/watch?v=xIQIWso_Lf0&list=PLxnKdJPwhDAi3FfIDqHbZU4v-liPc9k6M
Writing courses and events https://writingwestmidlands.org/

Getting your writing seen and heard

BBC Upload – upload your audio/video for radio https://www.bbc.co.uk/programmes/p07xtgyr
Fire and Dust poetry open mic – every first Thursday of the month, 7.30pm, hosted on Zoom. Find gigs on Facebook or Eventbrite. Free, but registration required. Everyone welcome: poets/spoken word artists, poetry fans and the poetry-curious.
Here Comes Everyone. An indie literary magazine based in Coventry. It publishes poetry, prose and visual art www.hcemagazine.com
Poetry gig guide and news https://www.writeoutloud.net/

Lightning Source UK Ltd.
Milton Keynes UK
UKHW021340131220
375041UK00006B/252

9 781911 048480